FREEDOM
— THE —
NEW HERESY

Adam, Where Are You?

D. Higgs

FREEDOM
— THE —
NEW HERESY

CONTENTS

This book is dedicated to…

the single greatest influence on my life, my Grandma, Mabel Higgs. Everything I am or could have ever imagined being, I owe to her. It was my Grandma who told me, "If you're going to lead the people, make sure you tell them the truth!" This book would not be possible without her. Love you, Grandma, eternally! This one's for you!

Freedom, the New Heresy was inspired by…
my brother, Donald Nakia Porter, one of the most amazing individuals to ever enter my life. Losing his life changed the trajectory of my own. My Ace taught me how to ask questions. It has been twenty-five years since he died, and he still keeps me asking questions. Bro, till I see you again, I love you more every single day!

FOREWORD

IN MERCURIAL TIMES, love always raises a voice that settles the hearts of men who have ears to hear the truth of its message. D. Higgs has been tempered through the fires of abuse, loss, ridicule, and control, all while never losing hope to experience true freedom.

All orthodoxy was once heretical, but it was by the bravery of a few men to carry out a message of liberty in the face of institutionalized manipulation that freedom was birthed. Those who live Godly lives will suffer persecution. Just like his predecessors—Martin Luther King Jr., Malcolm X, and Yeshua—D. Higgs was born for the express purpose of delivering the message of the divine's love through freedom. We are free to create and co-create, free to live and experience, free to express all that lies within.

Freedom, the New Heresy is a new epistle written by a modern-day Apostle, who is disconnected from the Establishment's limited perspectives. Take this journey through cognitive dissonance into clarity and strength. *Freedom, the New Heresy* comes with a new set of rules and responsibilities, but the rewards are well worth the adjustments that must be made. It will challenge you to change, it will stimulate you to grow. As you read *Freedom, the New Heresy*, enjoy the journey of becoming.

Jamel Lewis
Brooklyn, New York

INTRODUCTION

I HAVE OFTEN WONDERED if I sat down to write a book, what would I write about? What is it about my life that I would really want someone to know at this point? I'm guessing that's why it's taken me so long to actually sit and make the attempt. Oh, by the way, excuse me if it sounds like I'm just writing the thoughts as they're coming to my mind, because I *am!* I would much rather move out of the way and let it flow naturally. And I'll worry about the mistakes during the editorial process.

Right now, I actually feel that I'm in the perfect place and space in time to pen the thoughts and concepts that are currently shaping my life. I'm in such a place in my existence that past events and circumstances have all but faded from my memory. And those past ideologies and experiences have produced what I call a more evolved authentic version of myself. Over time, I have honestly detached emotionally from those many horrific experiences and ideologies that once shaped my life. And gratefully, I can now say, through those experiences, that I have become a more spiritually inclined and organic version of myself.

So, in attempting to decide what would be the central idea I wanted to write about, to debut as an author and to express my present state of being, I found only one word that continued to infiltrate and penetrate my mind and experience. That word was *freedom*. Hence, the title *Freedom, the New Heresy!* Hopefully, I can effectively navigate my readers through my own personal "journey to freedom!"

I want to be able to walk you through this journey, not as a literary artist attempting to dazzle you with words or intellectual prowess. I'm more concerned that my candor and transparency serve to help you to see *yourself* more clearly. I say that in all sincerity because, throughout these next pages, I hope to remind you who you really are. Trust me, I was blown away by how much I didn't truly know or understand about myself—and how amazed I was to find out that what I was searching for my entire life was already with me and within me.

Like so many others, I lived a counterfeit, nonproductive life and possibly possessed the lowest self-esteem you could ever imagine. I know! By now you're wondering what in the world does any of this have to do with freedom? And I'm sure you're wondering why I am referring to freedom as "the new heresy." Just give me a few minutes of your time, and I promise to lay it all out for you.

Now, before we go into whatever it is that spirit wants to say through me, I guess I should lay out a brief disclaimer, which hopefully will help you to understand me and what it is I am attempting to express. At the present time, if I had to consider myself anything, it would simply be a spiritual life coach.

However, I'm not in any way attempting to force any ideas or belief systems on anyone. I'm also not in any way concerned about what your religious affiliation is. Nor will I attempt to give you one. The only thing that I pray you believe in after reading this book is *yourself*. The only thing I want you to discover in this book is who you really are. As for me, my spiritual journey started off in a religious and dogmatic sect of Christianity.

With that said, I may use Biblical references—but don't run away just yet. Trust me, I have no desire to punish you with the Bible. Nor am I trying to get you to believe in it. Any references to Biblical stories will only give you insight into how my whole view of life and self was jaded by others' interpretations. Hopefully, the Biblical stories will shed light on interpretations that may be hindering you from living your best life.

I am not attempting to create a doctrine. Nor am I attempting to sabotage anyone else's beliefs. I'm only going through my own "journey to freedom"! I only want to share what I've learned on this journey about what was always present in me. Believe me, it wasn't necessarily a pleasant journey. But without a doubt it was definitely a fulfilling one—because, through it all, my memory kicked in and reminded me of who I *am*!

Now I'm able to live out who I am in the world and express myself in a way that reflects my higher self. Let's go into Chapter 1 together to see what Spirit wants to reveal to us.

CHAPTER 1

The Mastery of Misinterpretation

Misinterpretation is the most deadly of human sins.

—Lester del Rey

FREEDOM IS THE state of being free or at liberty rather than in confinement or under physical restraint. Personal liberty is opposed to bondage or slavery. *Freedom*, *independence*, and *liberty* refer to an absence of undue restrictions and an opportunity to exercise one's rights and powers.

I thought I should define the word *freedom* to start with, so that we're all on the same page. I'm sure, in all of our minds, we have already had some fundamental understanding of the term. When I hear the word *freedom*, I literally imagine infinity. Infinity in my mind represents no limits, no boundaries, and no restrictions. I must admit that this was not always my understanding of the word or the concept of being free. On the contrary, my understanding of freedom has vastly grown throughout the years.

Freedom may just be one of the most elusive concepts for humanity, even today, here in "the land of the free and the home of the brave." When we hear the word *freedom* or see its definition, we understand the idea cognitively or have some concept of its nature. But do we really understand it experientially? I promise you, a fundamental understanding of personal freedom pales in comparison to a true, organically lived free life.

For the record, I should have started out by informing you that when I speak of freedom, I'm not merely speaking about the rights we have as citizens of a nation, such as the right to vote or to speak openly. I'm talking about freedom on a much deeper level—freedom in a real, viable, spiritual way: the freedom and liberty that is the very makeup and core of our divine being.

I have always admired the courage of civil rights leaders who championed the cause of the oppressed and the enslaved. Such leaders come in all shapes, sizes, races, backgrounds, and sexual orientations, but the common ground for the marches, sit-ins, shutouts, protests, and uprisings has been the cries of the oppressed and the disenfranchised.

When a people tire of being oppressed, something rises up on the inside that says, "I will no longer be a slave, nor will I continue to be a victim." Now, again, I'm talking about freedom on a whole other level—freedom that is even deeper than the right to be a race of people or a specific sexual orientation. I'm talking about a freedom that, once it is realized, will shift the very course of your life as you know it. I am talking about the freedom to be the expressed image of God on the Earth. Remember, I told you that I would be sharing with you intricate parts of my journey to freedom, so I guess we should start there.

Why did I need a journey to freedom? What was it that enslaved me? What did I need to be free from? Are we all on a journey to freedom? Is that journey only necessary for a specific group of people? Those are just a few questions I thought I should ask, and maybe even attempt to answer.

In my forty years, I never knew that I was actually on a journey to find freedom. Truthfully, I had no idea that I was a slave. How could I know that I was a slave when I only knew what I knew, and assumed that all the information I had ever heard about myself was true?

Let's pause for a moment. In your own personal life, have you ever considered any of the following questions?

Are you a slave? What do you really know about yourself? Have you ever truly stopped to consider the things you've been taught about "yourself"? Are you a prisoner of another person's concepts and ideas about yourself?

Again, I really can't stress enough that I never knew that I was literally on a journey to freedom. I knew instinctively that something was missing from the story of my life, but I had no idea what it was.

James Allen has said, "You are today where your thoughts have brought you; you will be tomorrow where your thoughts take you."

Remember, I told you that I grew up in a very strict sect of Christianity—a Pentecostal Church experience that infused my emotions, but never stimulated my intellect. That is probably the most prominent of all my experiences, because Christianity influenced every aspect of my life. I lived by its rules and wandered aimlessly under its teachings, never even considering if it were intellectually sound or not.

You see, in most religious settings, intellect and wisdom are not necessary tools to climb the ladder of religious hierarchy. In fact, in many cases, using intellect and wisdom in religious settings is frowned upon and discouraged, and any thought outside of accepted doctrine is considered "heresy."

I will return to dealing with heresy in a moment. I intentionally entitled this chapter "The Mastery of Misinterpretation." It may sound awesome, but it's actually a simple concept that I want you to consider. Many of the ideas and values that we hold true and allow to shape our lives are usually the concepts and ideologies of other people. Our parents, teachers, religious leaders, and politicians influence the way we think and see the world around us.

But how often, if ever, do we stop to seriously consider those ideas and concepts—especially those ideas and concepts that tend to shape the way we see ourselves? I'm not asking these questions because I'm attempting to prove that the influential people in our lives are bad people, or prevaricators, or tyrants, or devils. On the contrary, I simply want you to begin to consider any ideology or system of belief that you hold as truth, and ask yourself: Does it truly serve your higher self?

Okay, now that we've got that out of the way, back to "The Mastery of Misinterpretation." Nothing has shaped my life more than the Biblical story of Adam and Eve. This was more than just an ancient story that was rehearsed in my imagination. Rather, the story literally shaped the way I viewed myself and the world around me. The story of Adam and Eve, taught to me through Christianity, revealed all that was wrong with human beings and just how horrific they are.

According to Christian teachings, Adam and Eve represented why human beings are unworthy of God or His benefits. Christianity taught me that Adam and Eve disobeyed God in such a way that every individual who came after them—including you and me—was doomed to a terrible fate, especially if we didn't accept Christianity's interpretation of the solution to the Adam and Eve problem. When I was a child, this story was the first to create in my awareness a concept of separation from God.

Somehow, that separation gave religion just the right amount of control to get me back in line and in touch with God. All I needed to do was subscribe to Christian beliefs, doctrines, and codes of ethics, follow them to the letter, and somehow I would mysteriously be reconciled with God, so that all my sins and wrongdoings would vanish.

Knowing that I was separated from God, thanks to Adam and Eve's disobedience, created within me an insatiable desire to fix my human dilemma by any means necessary. So, quite naturally, I followed to the best of my abilities the teachings of the church all the way up the ranks to Senior Pastor. Yes, me! Between the ages of 19 and 30, I was a Senior Pastor of three churches. But there was only one problem. The interpretation of the story of Adam and Eve presented a serious issue for me.

The problem was that, no matter how hard I worked, or how many rules I attempted to follow, I still somehow always ended up falling short in my attempts to reach God and to measure up to His standards. No matter how high I reached, I could never measure up. Unfortunately, Adam and Eve's disobedience was more powerful in my life than the rules provided by the church, for my interpretation of that disobedience kept me separate from God.

First of all, it continuously revealed to me my diabolical human dilemma, which was the fact that I, like Adam, was inadequate because of my sins. But was I *really* separated from God? Or did someone else's misinterpretation of that story create my illusion of separateness from God? I'm not sure that I can adequately express how devastating it was for me to discover that the very ideas I thought were leading me to the Way were actually standing *in* my way.

For many years of my life, I allowed others' interpretations to shape my life and the way I viewed the world around me. You see, from those interpretations, I not only learned my foundational Christian doctrines, teachings, and dogmas, but I also learned what I then considered my identity. This is "the mastery of misinterpretation"—that is, how we can hold onto an idea as truth without ever examining it through the lenses of logic and reason.

How often in everyday conversations do we misinterpret something that's being said and build an entire scenario around what we thought was true, later to discover that we had created a reality that did not in fact exist? Sadly, one of our greatest misinterpretations is of ourselves, when we gather the wrong information about ourselves and live a fraudulent and unfulfilled life.

Now, I know you don't think I would share with you how I directed my life based on my misinterpretation of Adam and Eve, and not give you a glimpse into how I've evolved in my understanding of that story. In fact, I can't wait to share with you how clearly I now view my life through the context of Adam and Eve. However, you have to keep reading, because this chapter is now over.

CHAPTER 2

A Delusional Self-Image!

Don't spend your life believing a story about yourself that you didn't write, that's been fed to you that simply you've accepted, embedded and added to. Let the story go, and there beneath is the real you... and your unique gifts, heart, and path that await you.

—Rasheed Ogunlaru

I BRIEFLY GAVE YOU an overview in Chapter 1 of how I once viewed myself, based on the misinterpretation of a fundamental Christian belief about the most familiar story known to man, Adam and Eve. It's a story that so many before me have used as philosophy, as well as in countless discussions and theories about how all of life began.

We've had sempiternal debates and theologica1781 arguments derived from the story of Adam and Eve. Many people like myself have lost themselves in history's misconceptions surrounding that story. And so many fraudulent identities have been created in the attempts to fit and to fix the delusional self-image that we've derived from our limited understanding of that story.

As I said earlier, I'm not in any way trying to convince you of any new doctrine or philosophy as it relates to Biblical text. The story of Adam and Eve may have had a huge effect on your life, or it may have had no bearing on your life at all. I only want to challenge you to see yourself as you should, so that you will understand, regardless of what fundamentalist religious organizations may think, that you are definitely not a mistake!

I simply would like to reveal to you how I used the same story that created a delusional self-image in my awareness to awaken a truth that I knew instinctively, but not cognitively. I would later discover through this story the truth that I now know experientially. Again, I had no idea that I was even on a journey to freedom. That awareness only came when I realized that the image I had of myself no longer served me, and how much of a slave I was to its misinterpretations.

I was forced to leave my religious confines to get a clearer understanding of what and who God truly is— and who She truly is to me, without religion's influence over how that relationship should go. I somehow knew instinctively that I would have to get rid of all the middlemen. No more interference was allowed. I needed to experience and understand God in a "real" and "practical" way.

The delusional self-image I had of myself continued to manifest in my mind every negative thing I had been taught to feel about myself—all based on an antiquated understanding of Adam and Eve. I could no longer hold beliefs that wouldn't allow room for intellect and reason. After all, what is the purpose of two such powerful tools if they are only good to defend my faith, but never to challenge it—especially when it is those beliefs that are creating the friction within my experiences?

On that faithful day in the garden, Adam did not just represent himself. According to traditional church teachings, he represented every man after him. Adam's fall from God's grace was a poison that entered into man's bloodstream, and its DNA can now be found in every one of our cells. Adam's disobedience brought with it sin and shame. And the effects of sin were so strong that they separated all of mankind from God, their creator. At least, that's the way most Christians are taught to view the story.

Isn't it weird that one of a man's sperm cells beats out millions of others to land on an egg that will turn into a human being? Yet, according to a fundamental church teaching, that human being is a sinner? If you don't agree with that conclusion, you could land in Hell.

Ironically, this human condition is not even of your own doing, but was caused by someone else's actions centuries before you even showed up. In the process of conception, you exhibited everything that proves that you're a born winner because that one sperm won the race. Yet, one of the first stories you will ever hear about the creation of our species is one of utter defeat.

Yeah, I know! It sounds utterly ridiculous to me as well, now that I've included logic and reason in my understanding of the story.

In Chapter1, I asked the question, "Am I separate from God? Or do I simply have a warped perception of myself, based on misinterpretation?

Of course, as we have discovered, the awareness I had of myself was delusional, because I allowed myself to shut off two of the most powerful tools loaned to man—logic and reason. Without those tools, I was forced to meander in the illusions of other men's opinions and interpretations.

When logic and reason began to contribute to my understanding of the story, the image I had created of myself began to vanish, and I discovered what true freedom really is! By discovering who I really am, I also discovered why any knowledge of true freedom would be considered heresy by religious authorities. I understand now why everything in our society is set to affirm and reaffirm the negative self-image that we have of ourselves.

You will be surprised, I'm sure, by just how much control we have relinquished to other people's ideas and opinions about who we are. In other words, we have allowed many outside influences to shape our lives without ever discovering the right questions to ask. Anyone who has broken free from religious dogmatic control has come to realize that God is found in the questions one asks. But we have been manipulated into believing that we should never question God. Actually, you were taught to never question other people's *interpretations* of God!

Let's now shift our understanding of the creation story. But before we begin, I should inform you that you will need to activate your logic and your reasoning skills, so that you can come along on this journey to discover your own personal freedom. Once again, I am *not* going to attempt to convince you of any new truths. I'm just going to give you a little push to reexamine your own truths.

"In the beginning," we find God going about His business of creation. We are introduced to an idea of God as a masterful creator, one who speaks through eternity and whose very words take on shape and life. According to the Biblical text, this God begins His conversation with man by revealing that He expresses Himself creatively. And He does not just create aimlessly. He is intentional and strategic in His plans, creating everything on purpose and with purpose, and seeing that purpose through till the end.

Now that this God has demonstrated His creative ability by giving shape to the universe as we perceive it today, He really starts to show off by taking the dust from the earth and shaping it to create His most prized creation, man! God is so serious about this creation that the Biblical text states that he created man "in His own image and likeness" (Genesis 1:27). Not only was God strategic in what He wanted man to look like, but He specifically wanted man to look like Him. Everything God is, man would become in one "breath." In that one breath, God placed into man's nostrils the same creative genius that God has himself.

Yes, you are a creative genius by design, and not by default. However, we use that creativity delusionally to create in our lives all the negatives that we experience. I am certain that before you finish reading this book, Spirit will help you to understand your creative genius a little better.

Once God created man, He put him to sleep like a skilled surgeon, took out his rib, and created woman.

So, let's review. First, God created the Heavens and the Earth. Then, from the dirt of the earth, He created man. Next, knowing that man did not want to be alone, He created a woman from man's rib. Have you noticed the progression? Everything that God made created from within itself another expression of God.

One touch, one word from God, literally had the power to produce and reproduce infinite expressions of itself in the universe, because nothing is born of God that does not bear the marks of God's DNA! This principle is lost in the story of Adam and Eve, and as a result, we have lost our true identity and taken on another.

But let me not get ahead of myself. (Slow down, playboy!) There is more logic and reason that we need to apply to this narrative, so that we will gain a clear understanding of the effects of living with a "delusional self-image."

God gave man dominion over all of the Earth, which we still have to this day. However, a clear understanding of this dominion principle is hidden amid the debris of Adam's misinterpretations and misrepresentations. Adam was given only one command: "You can eat from any tree in the garden, except from the Tree of the Knowledge of Good and Evil. Don't eat from it. The moment you eat from that tree, you're dead" (Genesis 2:16-17).[1]

This command is where it gets a little hairy for many people, because it is this instruction that began the delusional false image that I, among many others, created for myself. Undoubtedly, many people knowingly or unknowingly have derived a negative delusional self-image from this simple instruction, because this is the first story we've ever encountered that explains how we began as a species.

Undeniably, my delusional self-image started with a delusional image of God. I was taught to see and experience God all wrong. A delusional self-image is a direct result of a delusional God image. And vice versa, a delusional God image will definitely result in a delusional self-image. They are one and the same.

---

[1]   Unless otherwise indicated, all quotations from the Bible in this book are from the Message Bible.

Remember, everything that God created can reproduce itself, but that reproduction is still nothing but God! We are never *not* in a state of creation, even when we don't realize that we're creating our own experience. Just hang on; we will deal with that a little more in a moment.

The prohibition to eat from the Tree of the Knowledge of Good and Evil was an instruction that God clearly gave to Adam. Yet, for centuries, we have declared that Adam disobeyed God and ate of the tree anyway. From that disobedience, the church believes, sin entered the world, and all of mankind is now born into sin. Once again, I am asking you to activate a bit of logic and a tangible degree of reason to look at this story objectively.

A talking serpent seduces Eve to eat of the tree, which she and Adam had been absolutely forbidden to partake of. That single act is now known as the "Fall of Man." That is when man proved how diabolical he is, creating the doctrine that we are separate from God.

We have now seen how man fell from God's amazing grace. Or at least that's what we've been taught. But was that really a fall? Or was it simply a shift in the way that Adam and Eve perceived themselves?

I know that many of you may be ready to throw away this book as I teeter on the verge of heresy, but stick with me for just a moment. There are a few questions that we have to ask ourselves to fully understand the truest and purest way to see who we really are.

If Adam and Eve disobey God's command not to eat from the Tree, they are already sinful by disobeying—which means that sin existed *before* they ate from the Tree?

Houston, we have a problem!

Seeing the Genesis story in this way will force us to shift how we view the life and purpose of Jesus as well. If we are truly honest with ourselves, many of us have fostered an unhealthy relationship with Jesus, while never having an actual experience with the Truths that Jesus came to teach.

Let's go back to the Tree of the Knowledge of Good and Evil. Notice that this was *not* the *Tree* of Good and Evil, but the Tree of the *Knowledge* of Good and Evil. That means that good and evil already existed before Adam and Eve ate from the tree, because you can't have knowledge of something that doesn't already exist.

Contrary to the teachings of the church, Adam and Eve did not produce evil, or sin, through a single act of disobedience. They simply awakened what was already in them from the beginning. And we can find that same truth in ourselves.

Adam and Eve did not create good and evil. We have to credit God for that. Oh, my! I know I have committed heresy with such an ungodly accusation. Maybe you will accept it in God's own words:

> *I form the light, and create darkness: I make peace, and create evil: I the LORD do ALL these things.* (Isaiah 45:7)

(How much of ALL is ALL?)

Now we're back where we started with the original question. Was eating the fruit of the Tree truly a fall or only a shift in self-perception that would cause human beings to walk in an aimless pursuit of God in outside sources? There is no such thing as separation from God, except through our own thoughts and beliefs.

If good and evil existed before human beings were aware of them, *where* did they exist? By now, we can hopefully see that they already existed in man as a result of his design, and not as a result of a fall.

For decades, I assumed that due to man's fall, God was attempting to restore us back to our original state. In other words, due to man's egregious mistake, he is now deficient and separated from God. But with a new pair of eyes and a decade's worth of experience, I can now conclude that God never changed my design. Rather, I changed my perception of myself after abandoning a delusional self-image. In the past, I lived in a mold that had been created for me, without my permission and beyond my control.

I know that for many readers, this understanding will appear to be nothing more than heresy and unfounded rhetoric—a New Age ploy to get you to believe false doctrines and hearsay. I totally understand that, because I understand how a delusional self-image works. You see, in our minds, it is easy for us to accept that Adam and Eve were flawed and deserved death for being abominable creatures.

But to see them in the light of truth offends us. A delusional self-image will always distance us from any idea that we are divine. A delusional self-image will only allow us to believe the worst in us and not the best, or the "Greater Within Us."

Notice how immediately after Adam and Eve eat of the Tree, they put fig leaves over their nakedness (Gen. 3:7), literally making themselves like a tree. That is what a delusional self-image will do.

Millennia later, mankind is doing the same thing! Dressing, thinking, and acting like the source of new information about themselves, totally afraid to return to their natural, shameless, naked state before God. We are too afraid that God cannot handle what He has already seen and *knows!* We are afraid of what She designed within us in love and through LOVE!

This new shift in man's perceptions of himself now placed God in Heaven and man on Earth. Man lost his understanding of God by losing his understanding of *himself!* Once again, the concept of separation from God came as a result of man's delusional self-image. That is where the idea of doing something to please God was birthed. Religion is not God's plan to redeem man! Religion is a practice of the delusional self-image that man created as an occupation for himself—working by the sweat of his brow to reach God and to measure up to Her standards.

I know this may come as a surprise, but a part of our delusional self-image is thinking that we have to be a *part* of something, or identify with something, to give ourselves value. So, if you are not allowed to call yourself something, and someone else something else, how will you identify yourself? This separation is lived out in every area of our lives. We are now forced to see and identify others based on the labels that we have created, and not on the divinity from which we all stem!

Wow! Can you see just how deadly this concept is that you have allowed your delusional self to create for you? And can you see your continued lack of knowledge and understanding that keeps you perpetually repeating the cycle of living separately and divided?

It is no one else but ourselves who have created this false concept of God, and religion has carried out the duties and responsibilities of informing this dumbed down version of self. I know that may sound foreign, but remember, I'm merely describing my own journey to freedom. God was honest when He informed man that "If you eat its fruit, you are sure to die!" Because certainly a death had occurred. Man had now begun his journey through life, believing that he is separate from God. And separation from God is death. To believe that God is above and you are below, hoping that you will stumble on the right concept of God to deliver you from your horrifying human condition, will only damn you to Hell.

Let's not forget that if you don't make the right selection, Hell is certainly where you could end up. Do you at least see and identify the horrible manner in which we are now forced to view God? Through our misinterpretations and misrepresentations, this distorted view of God has become a concept that has infiltrated our thoughts, minds, practices, and behaviors.

We continue to manifest the condemnation we feel we deserve from this false concept of God. Don't forget that our creative intrinsic genius is always at work, even when we are not aware of it. So, if our belief does not serve us (because belief is simply an idea or concept that we continuously rehearse), we should get rid of it and find one that allows us to see ourselves connected to the Source!

God's Plan in Action!

Hopefully, you can see by now that Adam and Eve never exhibited any behaviors that were not organically a part of their makeup or design. We have discovered that good and evil were *not* the result of some fall from God's grace, but were concepts that were already present within man. Of course, man operated before eating of the tree without any knowledge.

So, Adam had not planned to commit an offense. He was not choosing evil over good. He made a choice based on his lack of knowledge or experience. What we must also understand, if we want to be totally honest, is that Adam was never lied to by the serpent, either! Let's take a look at that.

> *The woman said to the serpent, "We may eat fruit from the trees in the garden, but God did say, you must not eat fruit from the tree that is in the middle [center] of the garden, and you must not touch it, or you will die…."*
>
> *"You will not certainly die," the serpent said to the woman. "For God knows that when you eat from it, your eyes will be opened, and you will be like God, knowing good and evil."* (Genesis 3:2-5).

What the serpent said was not a lie. The serpent actually told Adam and Eve the truth, which was that their eyes would be opened and they would realize the truth of their own divinity. Are you still not convinced of that? Maybe it's too hard a pill to swallow? Well, let's look at what God said in the same chapter:

> *And the Lord God said, "The man has now become like one of us, knowing good and evil."* (Genesis 3:22)

In this statement, God confirms what the serpent had already revealed to Adam and Eve. Don't you find it strange that God does not say that man is like Him until man falls? Why does the fall reveal man's divinity, yet, before he eats of the tree, he is never referred to as being like God, with the exception of when God creates man in His own image. And we somehow believe that we lost that identity during that so-called fall. We also believe that by adopting some sort of religious philosophy, we can rid ourselves of this evil sin problem. That is, following a system of laws, codes, and ethical principles will bring us closer to God.

I hope that you are able to see now that Adam's eating of the tree was not some accident that caught God off guard, sending Him into a panic to fix the problem. Such an idea would mess with the "sovereign" and "omniscient" power of God!

Is He or isn't He in full control? Certainly, we must give God credit for being a masterful creator, who set the stage and directed every scene. Contrary to the false delusional doctrines we have created surrounding this story, God's original plan was to start man on an amazing journey to discover true freedom and absolute liberty—if he would only open his eyes and follow the truth.

Did you get that? Hidden in this story is an amazing principle, one that I've learned on this amazing discovery to freedom, and one that we can see in this narrative. Adam and Eve did not disobey a command; they did what was logical to them. They followed the truth and sought wisdom. You see, logic and reason have always been present within man.

> In the beginning was the Word, the Word was
> with God and the Word was God. (John 1:1)

Word in this text means *logos*, which actually means logic. So, from the very beginning, logic was present and evident within man. Let's not forget that everything God created possesses within itself all of God's abilities. Man has within himself a natural sense to follow the truth, but he is taught to be afraid of that truth. Subconsciously, he was taught fear in the teachings of the church surrounding this story. Let's see how Genesis paints the picture of the serpent.

> Now the serpent was more crafty than any of
> the wild animals the Lord God had made. He
> said to the woman, "Did God really say, 'You
> must not eat from any tree in the garden?'"
> (Genesis 3:1)

In its very description, the serpent is considered crafty, yet this beast tells Adam and Eve the truth about the tree, and also informs them that they will be just like God. Once we apply logic and reason to this story, are we to assume that the talking serpent just *happened* to be on the forbidden tree?

Clearly, this serpent was not Satan, "the Father of lies," who cannot tell the truth even if he wants to. The serpent not only tells Adam and Eve the truth, but reveals to them how to experience their full divinity. These are not attributes that we were taught to ascribe to Satan, right?

> *And when the woman saw that the tree was good for food, and that it was pleasant to the eyes, and a tree to be desired to make one wise, she took of the fruit thereof, and did eat, and gave also unto her husband with her; and he did eat.* (Genesis 3:6)

Notice how Eve does not act to disobey the directives of God, but purely from a desire for sustenance, beauty, and wisdom.

> *Above all and before all, do this: Get Wisdom! Write this at the top of your list: Get Understanding!* (Proverbs 4:7)

Pursuing wisdom and understanding has always been healthy. These powerful tools help us to navigate throughout life. Yet, on so many levels, we have chosen the dumbed down version of self, which chooses ignorance over wisdom and foolishness over understanding.

But I don't mean wisdom and understanding that come from books or mere academic achievements in the corridors of higher learning. I am talking about *spiritual* wisdom and understanding. They are what we have lost and refuse to return to. It has become easier for us to pass off our ignorance as intelligence. I am all for higher education. Many educated people have made excellent accomplishments, and that is to be commended. However, we are often quick to study everything outside ourselves, while never taking the time to "let a man examine himself" (1 Cor. 11:28).

CHAPTER 3

The Tree of the Knowledge of Good and Evil!

In each of us, two nations are at war—the good and the evil. All our lives the fight goes on between them, and one of them must conquer. But in our own hands lies the power to choose— what we want most to be, we are.

—Robert Louis Stevenson

I THINK THERE IS something so interesting about the story of Adam and Eve that somehow has gone ignored in our religious details. Have you ever noticed that good and evil exist simultaneously in the Tree of Knowledge? How has religion somehow managed to take on a mission to control good in the world, while constantly reminding people about everything that is evil about the world?

It seems strange to me that religion has somehow ignored the fact that the knowledge of *both* good and evil was forbidden. Good was not recommended or required over evil. Nor was good singled out as having more value than evil. According to the traditional teachings of religion, especially Christianity, we must deduce that if Adam and Eve were forbidden to become evil people, they were also forbidden to become good people, since both good and evil existed on the same tree.

This point may seem insignificant to religious people, but it is not. This point underlies how we see ourselves and our relationship with God, divinity, and the Adam and Eve story. Not seeing this point has literally hindered us from seeing the world as it is.

This missing link to the truth about good and evil has caused us to judge some people as worthy of God's grace and mercy and others as unworthy. It is no longer God who gives us our identity, but instead we are identified by where we fit in our conceptions of good and evil. Hopefully, we can get a clearer understanding of the mysteries of the Tree's design, which will enable us to change how we see ourselves, in turn which will change how we see and treat the other people on the planet.

Again, the knowledge of good and evil existed simultaneously within the makeup of the Tree's design. Now that we know this, we can see clearly that good and evil cannot exist without each other. We cannot know good unless we know evil, and we cannot know evil unless we know good. Neither of them should be feared or revered above the other, since neither can exist without the other. They are both necessary to have an authentic encounter with God.

God is not simply trying to get us to a specific destination; rather, She is longing to live *through* us and *as* us. When you see good and evil as one, you find the beauty and wisdom within them, and begin to realize their purpose in your life. Let's look at this a little more.

> *When the woman saw that the fruit of the*
> *tree was good for food and pleasing to the eye,*
> *and also desirable for gaining wisdom, she*
> *took some and ate it.* (Genesis 3:6)

Why is it that when Eve looked at the Tree for what it truly was, she only saw its benefits, and not the delusional self-image created from partaking of it? Adam and Eve's view of the Tree changed only when they became aware of the things that differentiated good from evil.

One sinister human misconception is thinking that it is our job to identify all of the good and evil within other people. Depending on how we measure the things that differentiate good from evil, we determine other people's value. But, trust me, we are almost always wrong in our perceptions and assumptions.

In truth, most of our misconceptions surrounding good and evil are based on our misinterpretations of the Adam and Eve story. We have even created labels to identify specific qualities that can help us to brand someone as good or evil. Before Eve eats from the tree, she sees wholeness in it. But after Adam and Eve eat from the Tree together, they are introduced to the idea of separation from God.

Eve sees wisdom in the Tree when she sees it as a whole. We have already seen in previous chapters that good and evil existed in people before they ate from the Tree. That eating simply produced *knowledge* of what existed from the beginning. In other words, Adam and Eve had no awareness of what was present in them from the beginning, but after they ate from the Tree, all of that changed.

It had to be a terrifying experience for them to have their eyes opened to more information than they could ever have imagined. Mind you, nothing changed in their environment. Everything was the same as it had always been from the beginning. But they now had new information about themselves, and that new information shifted the way they saw themselves.

We also saw earlier that eating from the Tree was not some mistake that forfeited everything that God had intended for man, although that is the basis for most fundamental religious teachings. Clearly, eating from the Tree was no mistake, nor was God a bit surprised. Rather, that was the beginning of a beautiful journey for man—the journey to freedom that I have mentioned regarding myself.

Adam and Eve started man on a journey that we're still traveling today. And our experiences only serve to remind us of who we are in God and "Her" original purpose for our lives—which was for us to be individual creative expressions of God on Earth.

But so many people have abolished or distorted this journey to conform to the many false images that society and religion have created for us in a failed attempt to control man's horrific human dilemma. And reinforcing man's delusional self-image has become an extremely lucrative business, I might add.

Good and evil are *not* two separate ideas. They are the same idea. They are one. Our measure of good and evil should not be to determine whether or not we're in right standing with God, as if She would punish us more for one thing than another. Everyone or everything that we have perceived as good has not necessarily been good for us. Nor have those whom we perceived as evil necessarily been evil for us. How often do some of the most horrific experiences end up producing some of the greatest outcomes?

If an experience is bad, but the outcome is good, is the whole of the experience good or bad? Or, if the experience is good and the outcome is bad, does the bad outcome alter the good experience? The answer totally depends on how the individual has perceived the experience.

We miss out on the obvious when we remove logic and reason from our interpretations of the Adam and Eve story. If God only made good, how would we know that it was good? We would have nothing to compare it to. And this idea that God made *both* good *and* evil really scares us, so in our depiction of this narrative, we have the serpent to blame for all of the evil in the world. In fact, we have needed Satan for centuries to be a scapegoat for our delusional self-image. If we can blame the serpent, we no longer have to take responsibility for our own lives and experiences.

The serpent has become our comfort zone. Indeed, the serpent has given us more faith and headlined more sermons than God has. You see, the moment man began to operate in this delusional self-image, he began the blame game. Eve blames the serpent, and Adam blames the woman God gave him. This story differs little from human behavior today. We blame everyone and everything else for the distorted perceptions we have of ourselves.

> *Immediately the two of them did see what's really going on—saw themselves naked! They sewed fig leaves together as makeshift clothes for themselves.* (Genesis 3:7)

This fall in consciousness is exactly when we started to play dress-up—that is, when we began to create standards for one another. So, we didn't just change our clothes. Rather, we began to see the need for labels—and those labels allowed us to identify others on our scale of good and evil.

Labeling one another does not require genuine relationship. In fact, these labels prevent us from experiencing others spiritually. We can only identify one another materially, which creates divisions between us.

Our primitive perceptions of good and evil are at the core of this delusion. Dressing like the tree by putting on fig leaves created conformity.

When man began to control the concepts of good and evil, that created many wicked people who supposedly spoke in the name of God or in the name of their political parties. Those people institutionalized everyone else, making sure that they were following all the rules assigned to them.

Your fear that good and evil have separated you from God is just the right amount of control needed to allow middlemen to dictate your experience with God. It wasn't good and evil that scared Adam into hiding. It was his divinity that made him afraid. Similarly, we have allowed ourselves to be hypnotized under religion's control and dominance.

I cannot stress enough the amount of spiritual and material poverty we have accumulated over the past few centuries, due to our lack of understanding. The time has come for us to snap out of the egocentric idea that by our works, we can appease God. If we don't break free from that misunderstanding, we soon won't be able to compete for survival.

We have neglected our brilliance in mathematics, science, architecture, literature, art, and other creative pursuits in order to believe in a fraudulent concept of God. Due to that fall in consciousness, along with the help of evil systems and governments, the fight for real spiritual identity continues. But that is not won from the outside in. It's won from the inside out!

Adam, where are you? Enough with waiting for a leader, another Martin or another Malcolm. You are who God is looking for to inspire this generation, to reshape the brilliance of our design on Earth. Yes, you! When people begin to examine themselves, and see themselves worthy of God's best and as one with divinity and each other, then real change can happen!

We can spend an eternity placing blame on others, as we try to get them to like, respect, and validate us. Self-respect is an inside job that you have to do for yourself. When you truly get to the bottom of who you are, and stop hiding your brilliance and allowing fear to hinder you, you will begin to create for yourselves the lives you know you truly deserve. Because you will no longer settle for things that don't uplift you and bring you true freedom.

Seeing ourselves as we truly are will make us become wiser in the ways we spend, and where we spend. Seeing ourselves as we truly are will cause us to love our brothers and sisters, so that we only seek to build one another up, knowing that there is more than enough room for all God's children to succeed. Seeing ourselves as we truly are may just mean that we owe apologies to some people. And we need lots of forgiveness—mainly of ourselves.

Forgiveness and self-love are necessary for real reconciliation and repentance. That is how we grow and develop into a force within the global economy. I have no competition, nor am I anyone else's competition—not because I see myself as better than others, but because I only seek to live and walk out my own purpose. When we truly begin to see ourselves as we are, that robs us of nothing!

CHAPTER 4

"Adam, Where Are You?"

Not until we are lost do we begin to understand ourselves.

—Henry David Thoreau

I N MY OPINION, God asked Adam one of the most profound questions ever—a question that can literally be heard echoing throughout our current generation. Of course, God was asking a rhetorical question, since He is omniscient and already knows everything—including exactly where Adam was hiding, and why. "The eyes of the Lord," says the Proverb (15:3), "are everywhere."

God called to the Man: "Where are you?"

> He said, "I heard you in the garden and
> I was afraid because I was naked. And I hid."
> (Genesis 3:9-10)

God wasn't asking where Adam literally was. He was asking Adam where he saw himself in relation to the divine.

Once again, man's fall in consciousness created separation, for Adam believed that his new understanding separated him from God. And it did! Not because God lost sight of His perception of man. That's a blatant lie! God never lost sight of His plans for man. It was man who lost sight of God and separated himself from Him, for both Adam and Eve put on fig leaves to hide their nakedness.

God was asking Adam, "Where is your originality?"

That is exactly what modern-day religion attempts to suppress. Religion is a lie that teaches us to mask and dress up who we really are, in the belief that God cannot handle us. The truth is, it's *us* who can't handle the truth about ourselves. We would rather believe every lie that some outside influence has designed for us than take the time to truly answer this very old question? "Adam, where are you? Why are you still hiding in religion's dominance and control? Where is your nakedness? Where is your individuality and originality? Who robbed you of your brilliance?"

As I have stated from the start of this book, my interpretations of scriptures are just my attempt to clarify some major distortions. And even if I'm dead wrong in my solutions, I've certainly raised some questions that contradict our primitive beliefs. However, I am not merely trying to challenge religious people to see scriptures differently. If these verses have no impact on your life at all, I still want to challenge you to ask yourself, "Where am I?" You may have never set foot in a church or any other religious setting. That's all good and cool. But you can still ask yourself where you are in relation to the divine, or unconditional Love.

It's very easy for us to get lost in everyone else's ideas of who we are. So many people work at jobs they hate because they aren't maximizing their fullest potential. Some stay in "situationships" that completely contradict everything they are. Yet, they never ask themselves, "Where are we?"

We flock to churches every week, crying out to a God that we believe is outside of us, separate and distant, who judges and condemns the whole world. And we claim that we're free to worship! How can that be if we aren't even free to be ourselves?

We call worship intimacy with God. That's a brilliant way to describe it. However, at some point in an intimate relationship, you have to get naked. You have to come out of those clothes and expose everything to your partner. Every scar, every blemish, every stretch mark, every dark spot. All of it is out in the open. And any good lovers are totally blind to all the things in their partners that others might find unattractive.

If an ordinary lover can love so completely, then certainly we must assume that God, who is the very definition and expression of Love, certainly feels that way about every one of us. In fact, the shift in consciousness never happened with God. It was man who shifted his direction and attention away from the idea of God being *with* us to the notion of God being *above* us. That is also how we developed fear. God did not give us fear; we gave it to ourselves. As it says in 2 Tim. 1:7, "God did not give us the spirit of fear but power, and of Love and a sound mind."

Fear was created out of man realizing his own divinity. Don't forget that the serpent tells Adam and Eve that "they would be like God, knowing both good and evil." So it is good and evil that they now come to fear—and to this day, man is hiding, never facing his duality. He just looks for better ways, through religious servitude, to masquerade his duality as righteousness.

Let's quit blaming God for being in conflict with humanity because of good and evil. That isn't the truth. It's us who have lived for centuries in our delusion that good and evil separated us from God. We believed that we could control good and evil and manipulate them at our leisure, when in truth we could never know one without experiencing the other. How would you appreciate great days without experiencing "bad" ones?

Even when you choose to use your freedom in a negative way, the universe responds to that negativity and returns it back to you. The fear that man created for himself has created countless man-made systems of control to correct the problem of separation from God. Unscrupulous individuals realized long ago that they can manipulate and control others in the name of this delusion, and they have accumulated vast fortunes doing so.

Maybe we all must answer the question of "Where are we?" Perhaps we're all at different points and stages in our lives. I certainly remember when I was forced to face this question, and, like everyone else, I had to answer honestly. The truth is, I was hiding from myself, lost in my own delusions.

I was faced with this question shortly after a relationship ended. That time wasn't about anybody else, it was all about me, and I had to face the fact that I was hiding from the man I knew I could be—the man I should have been and deserved to be.

I can't play the role of victim as if I lost that relationship to some outside entity or mere infidelity. It was solely destroyed by my own ignorance and arrogant pride. Now, don't get me wrong, I'm truly grateful for the breakup, because I finally heard the question, "Where are you?" Because of the breakup, it was so loud and so clear. It led me to a new understanding of myself, and was also a pivotal experience on my journey to writing this book.

I allowed my identity to be developed by all the outside opinions about and influences on my life—even the negative ones that I developed about myself over time. I grew up around constant and consistent negativity and drama. As a child, I truly hated that, because I was very timid and shy. But growing up with negativity can easily carry on into your adult life. Before you know it, you've become the very things you hate the most.

Those negative childhood experiences, along with all the religious dogma and doctrines that controlled my life, created a sense of unworthiness and even self-hatred. I was literally a ticking time bomb, a complete and utter wreck, broken by and consumed with rage. And I took that out on the people who tended to care the most about me, never truly believing that I could be happy, healthy, whole, and in love.

And I mean a healthy, happy, and whole loving relationship with myself. Again, it was "Adam, where are you?" Not the me that I created for social media. Not the image I portrayed of a fabulous illusion of reality. Not the me that the institutional church or organized religion fashioned. Where was I? The me that I had been hiding from God, thinking that He couldn't handle me? The me that is really me without the mask? The me that is not concerned merely with being right? The me that sees the need for a moment to be real about myself?

The delusional self-image that we create about ourselves has us always feeling the need to judge and condemn others, while totally neglecting ourselves emotionally and psychologically, with an incessant senseless need to be in control. That can seriously and easily become too much of a task to handle.

How long will you hide from God, attempting to appease God through religious servitude, rituals, sacrifices, and services? How many "holy convocations" are enough before you finally please God?

> *"I can't stand your religious meetings. I'm fed up with your conferences and conventions. I want nothing to do with your religion projects, your pretentious slogans and goals. I'm sick of your fund-raising schemes, your public relations and image making. I've had all I can take of your noisy ego-music. When was the last time you sang to me? Do you know what I want? I want justice—oceans of it. I want fairness—rivers of it. That's what I want. That's all I want."* (Amos 5:21-24)

Within this generation, and within our entire culture, we have literally become a perversion. Religion is a form of immaturity, a choice to never grow past a remedial and fundamental understanding, to evolve to a more spiritually awakened people who live in and from their divinity. Most individuals, hypnotized in a state of religious servitude and false righteousness, have become so primitive in their understanding of this culture that they have no idea that this is the very last organized institutional church generation.

And most people are not even prepared for this shift, simply because they have deluded themselves into believing that people have fallen in consciousness. They don't know that there many people who are fully aware, fully alert, and fully centered in Christ Consciousness. Adam, where are you? How long will you hide yourself from divinity? How long will you have the form of Godliness while denying its power?

Jacob is another example of this egregious attempt to dress up to receive the promise, as opposed to living by faith and trusting God to work out all the details of the promise:

> *God told her, "Two nations are in your womb, two people butting heads while still in your body. One people will overpower the other, and the older will serve the younger."* (Genesis 25:23)

Jacob's life started out with the promise that he would be served by his older brother, Esau. Furthermore, he was a descendant of Abraham, the father of many nations, who had the ultimate promise over his life—a promise that covered Jacob and Esau, and also you and me. Just like Adam before him, when it came down to trusting God for the promise, and believing that God's promise was more than enough, Jacob played dress-up:

> *She [Rebekah, the mother of Jacob] took the goatskins and covered his hands and the smooth nape of his neck. Then she placed the hearty meal she had fixed and fresh bread she'd baked into the hands of her son Jacob. He went to his father and said, "My father!" "Yes?" he said. "Which son are you?" Jacob answered his father, "I'm your firstborn son Esau. I did what you told me. Come now; sit up and eat of my game so you can give me your personal blessing."* (Genesis 27:17-19)

Here Jacob has a promise over his life, which states that he will rule over his older brother, but his lack of trust in God creates an idea in him that his own identity and the promise are not enough to secure the blessing. So, he does what religion teaches all of us to do. He dresses up and pretends. That is why we are a generation that is led purely by feelings. Things have to feel good to us, or we don't sanction them as blessed. And we carry this feeling out in so many areas of our lives. That is why we have so-called spiritual leaders who can only stimulate us emotionally, while at no point stimulating us intellectually. The book of Genesis explains the problem to us:

> *When Isaac had become an old man and was*
> *nearly blind….* (Genesis 27:1)

Isaac, Jacob's father, is a representation of today's religious and political culture. Religious and political people today are old and nearly blind! They are primitive in understanding—an understanding that on so many levels has created many of our ills. And they are so blind that they refuse to see Spirit. That primitive understanding only allows room for judgments based on the flesh!

Isaac blesses the right child in the wrong moment all because of a feeling, and that is what we are literally doing today—blessing all the wrong things and people based on feelings, because they make us feel good without ever challenging forward progression and evolution. So many of us are blessing "situationships" just because they make us feel good, while ignoring all the negative damage being created by the reality of things.

> *Then you will experience for yourselves the*
> *truth [alítheia], and the truth will free you.*
> (John 8:32)

Alítheia means "truth," knowing "reality" over "illusion." For so many, illusion has been our reality, to the point that we honestly have no idea where to begin to face reality. We've been dressing up, trying to get God's attention through mass conformity, so we are truly afraid to embrace our realities. So many unhappy families stick together in illusion, instead of facing the reality of love by way of truth, growing and maturing beyond illusion, and developing that beautiful, natural, free-flowing version of self.

In the Biblical story, Jacob wrestles with an angel, saying, "I won't let you go till you bless me!" Yet, we never fully understood *why* Jacob was wrestling with the angel.

> *But Jacob stayed behind by himself, and a man wrestled with him until daybreak. When the man saw that he couldn't get the best of Jacob as they wrestled, he deliberately threw Jacob's hip out of joint. The man said, "Let me go; it's daybreak." Jacob said, "I'm not letting you go 'til you bless me." The man said, "What's your name?" He answered, "Jacob." The man said, "But no longer. Your name is no longer Jacob. From now on it's Israel (God-Wrestler); you've wrestled with God and you've come through."* (Genesis 32:24-28)

This wrestling was bigger than some material possession. The fight was not merely an attempt to get an angry brother off Jacob's back. Jacob didn't receive the blessing the moment Isaac laid hands on him. The blessing came from the encounter with Spirit. Jacob's name was changed, and he was given a new identity.

That is what living by faith is all about! It is hitting the refresh button and discovering yourself again, getting a new identity and a fresh perspective on your originality. I'm not talking about living the illusions of grandeur regardless of your economic status. I'm talking about getting to discover all the greatness that is you, without all of the outside noise and influences trying to shape and navigate your journey.

We have held people hostage to our primitive concepts of and dogmas about God, never allowing for freedom of infinite expression. This has made us cynical, judgmental, condescending, shady, and malicious toward one another, believing that we are robbed if we praise others for their accomplishments. We don't know that praising others is the only way we can successfully build relationships with one another.

FREEDOM THE NEW HERESY

> *If you've gotten anything at all out of following Christ, if his Love has made any difference in your life, if being in a community of the Spirit means anything to you, if you have a heart, if you care—then do me a favor: Agree with each other, Love each other, be deep-spirited friends. Don't push your way to the front; don't sweet-talk your way to the top. Put yourself aside, and help others get ahead.*
>
> *Don't be obsessed with getting your own advantage. Forget yourselves long enough to lend a helping hand.* (Philippians 2:1-4)

We are not the man-made labels that we have created for ourselves. We are bigger than those! I don't want to be forced to defend stereotypes that are based on our preconceived notions of a label. It would be so great to have genuine dialogues with people again without the need for pretense. Maturity accepts that everyone is different, period! And different doesn't mean bad or good! It just means different!

All souls have different experiences, and they perceive the world totally differently based on those experiences. It is not my job to judge those experiences or control them. I simply judge if the vibrations are loving, and that determines the connection. Love is a universal language because "Love is God!"

Time is waiting for your brilliance to arrive. This moment is waiting to hear your song! Creation is longing for your invention! Someone needs employment and a future at your company! Some classroom needs your brilliant lecture! Some stage needs to witness your art and creativity! Something brilliant is waiting for you to discover it!

You deserve a relationship that is loving, kind, and mature. As I said at the beginning of this book, you were no mistake. Everything that you needed to create the life that you desire, you brought here with you. But you will never fully discover that brilliance until you are truly ready to get centered and be honest with yourself about yourself. "Adam, where are you?"

Not only must we answer that question, but God also asked both Adam and Eve another very valuable question that I think we should briefly consider.

> *And he [God] said, "Who told you that you were naked? Have you eaten of the tree, whereof I commanded that you should not eat?"* (Genesis 3:11)

God had to ask this question after hearing Adam's shift in consciousness. Mankind had now seen himself as naked before God. But a nakedness that brought about guilt and shame. This was not the natural organic state of seeing oneself as whole and complete in God. Adam's source of information had now shifted, and Spirit needed to get to the bottom of who had told him this new information. Who or what was now shaping Adam's identity? Who was the source of this delusional self-image? Today, this question, "Who told you that you were naked?" still needs to be individually answered. Who have you been getting the information from that shapes your identity? Who taught you to see yourself the way you do?

Clearly, God knew that Adam had an outside source of information—in other words, that someone (the Serpent) outside of the manufacturer (God) was now speaking to the manufactured (Adam). And still today, outside sources and influences are shaping our realities. We have abolished the voice of the Creator and have become enamored with the voice of the created.

First, Adam dressed like the source of his new identity (the Tree), and then he began to speak like it. That is why both insiders (religious individuals) and outsiders ("sinners") can today be found dressing and speaking like the source of their new identity, while never knowing that they must eventually answer the question, "Who told you those things about yourself?"

Remember, Adam and Eve were not in a fallen state, as some religious people have told us. The first humans were experiencing their divinity for the very first time. Although they had separated from God in their understanding, they were no less divine. Because their separation was how they chose to view their freedom, the universe responded to the guilt and shame they felt. They began to shift the universe in the direction of their new thought.

And that shift occurred immediately after God asked them, "Who told you that you were naked?" God then cursed the Serpent for his role in the action, cursed women with birth pains, and cursed men with hard labor. The universe had to respond to the way they now perceived their relationship with God!

Your divinity does not cease to exist because you choose to dumb it down. On the contrary, Spirit is now simply forced to continue to respond to you, based on your delusion. Poverty, lack, sickness, disease, anger, bitterness, condemnation, judgment, wrath, greed, selfishness, and so on, are all the things we continue to manifest in our realities because we choose to see ourselves separate from the Source.

I could choose to live my life based on what other people think and feel about me being a black male, or what they feel about me being a black homosexual male. But if I allowed the opinions of outsiders to define my identity, that would cause me nothing but grief and shame. However, when I choose to see myself as a creative expression of my manufacturer's design, then that frees me to *be me!*—and without guilt, shame, or any fear.

The only time I've struggled with my identity was when I allowed outside influences (parents, family, friends, Christianity, society, and politics) to define and design my reality. That is why we have become a culture so consumed with the drama and negativity in other people's lives, which should teach us how much work we still need to do on ourselves. One of those things on that agenda should be answering the question, "Who told you that you were naked?"

CHAPTER 5

Getting Back to the Center!

*A mind at peace, a mind centered and not focused
on harming others, is stronger than any physical
force in the universe.*

—Wayne Dyer

I'M NOT CERTAIN what you're doing in the world at this very moment! It's May 5, 2016, *Cinco de Mayo*, and I'm up at 1:27 A.M.—writing, of course. And to be totally honest, I think the few paragraphs that I'm about to pen are possibly more important than all my other paragraphs combined—even though I believe those other paragraphs will serve to help you better understand your divinity. In fact, that's the only reason for this book in the first place.

By this point, I have shown you how my opinions and views surrounding Adam and Eve have changed dramatically over time—not to create a gospel or doctrine to support my current understanding, but as a *result* of my current understanding. Without a doubt, my original opinions, dogmas, and beliefs no longer served me or my life. I definitely needed a new set of eyes, so that I could see myself as I ought to.

Make no mistake about it, my need to see myself in a self-sabotaging manner took forty years to develop. I certainly had no respect for my divinity and no idea what spirituality really meant. Had I known, I would have treated people a whole lot better, because I would have treated *myself* better. I'm one of those individuals who found out through the school of hard knocks that it is impossible to love someone else if you don't first truly love *yourself*.

In the beginning of this book, I said that something was once clearly missing from my understanding of self. On this journey, I've learned finally what that something was. I was missing a positive self-image, which prevented me from truly loving myself. Like Adam, I somehow found myself deficient, and I grew up in a religious mindset that continued to reinforce the judgment that I was somehow inferior.

Loving yourself sounds so easy to do, but in truth it can be a daunting task in today's culture, because everything is set in motion to point out all the things that reaffirm our critical self-image. That self-image says you are deficient, inadequate, not enough. That's such a horrific lie being sold to you, and it definitely is not the way God sees you.

You were adequate from the moment you agreed to step into time. Everything else, no matter what anyone else says, is a lie! A huge boldfaced lie! Yes, right now, in whatever condition you may find yourself, you are more than enough! You are more than adequate! You are wonderfully designed! The only things that hinder you from seeing that are the false perceptions of self that were given to you by others.

Changing the way you think God perceives you is as simple as changing the way you see yourself. I grew up under a Christian idea that portrayed God in Heaven viciously watching everything that we ever do in life and then punishing us for it. The moment I stepped out of character, I would be forced to face His wrath. In that portrait, God was a tyrant who caused earthquakes, famines, tsunamis, and all manner of vindictive destruction when He didn't get His way.

That delusional God image not only resulted in me seeing myself in a negative way, it also caused me to falsify my love for Him and myself. In all of my years as a Bible thumper and hell and brimstone preacher, I realized I never got to love God fully or truthfully. I feared Him, and that fear was created because I thought of myself as deficient and fallen from His Grace. That is when I had to ask myself if that relationship with God was about me being right, without me ever getting the chance to be real.

I'm not talking about what society calls "being real" today, which means being rude and brash, which is nothing more than a cover-up for low self-esteem. I'm talking about being able to be real "naked and not ashamed" in the presence of God, living freely in your truth, whatever that truth may be—knowing that you're not some flawed, deficient being forced to walk in consistent condemnation of yourself. What a miserable existence it is to meander through life seeing yourself as never being enough. You struggle by the sweat of your brow to follow man-made rules and rituals, forced to always measure up to what you believe God wants and requires of you.

Now we see that religion is a failed attempt at restoring man's perceptions of God and self. Religion has become the very thing that has separated us from God, preventing us from having an authentic and organic relationship with Him. Men have placed rules and demands on you in the name of God. That has hindered you from living your greatest life.

In all of the years that I was under religion's spell, I never even *knew* God! How was that possible when I followed all the rules and committed myself to all the religious acts and dogmas? Easy! Because my attempting to keep those rules prevented me from having true experiences with the Source, the Infinite, God!

Through false worship, my emotions were stimulated, but without any true, natural, genuine experience with the God I claimed to worship. In those false worship experiences, I literally put out into the universe declarations of how unworthy I was of God and His Benefits. I cried and got emotional over the thought that God is a Supreme being in Heaven who requires me to tell Him how wonderful and awesome He is—all the while diminishing my own value and intrinsic worth.

That is such a false image of God! You truly tell Him how awesome and wonderful He is by knowing how wonderful and awesome *you* are!

But let's get back to the point of this chapter. Trust me, I haven't forgotten that this chapter is called "Getting

Back to the Center." So, let's get back to the center. The truth that we need to learn is such a powerful but hidden principle. It's one of those things that we see textually, yet not through real cognitive awareness. Let's look at it:

> *The Lord God made all kinds of trees grow out of the ground—trees that were pleasing to the eye and good for food. In the center of the garden were the tree of life and the tree of the knowledge of good and evil.* (Genesis 2:9)

Do you get it? Have you found the principle yet? Okay, let's add another verse to see if you can understand it more clearly:

> *When the Lord saw Moses coming to take a closer look, God called to him from the center of the bush, "Moses! Moses!" "Here I am!" Moses replied.* (Exodus 3:4)

We have possibly never even noticed that the geographical location of the Tree of Life and the Tree of the Knowledge of Good and Evil was given to us. And I'm sure many of us have never known that this was not some extra added detail without divine purpose.

It absolutely has a purpose, which is to show us where we can still find the Tree of Life and the Tree of the Knowledge of Good and Evil today!

We see the principle reinforced in the famous passage of Moses and the burning bush. Notice that Moses hears the voice of God in the middle or center of the bush. You want to know where *you* hear the voice of God? It's not through your ears. It's in the center of your very being! That's where God chooses to speak to and through you. Yes, life is found when you get to the center of yourself. But we're taught to be afraid of getting to the center of our being. However, that is where our understanding of ourselves is realized.

Moses heard God's voice from the center of the bush. That is still where we will find the voice of God today— at the center or core of our very being, when we finally take off all the masks and denounce all the outside voices.

Just as in the center of fruits there are the seeds that produced them, it's the same with us! When we get to *our* center, who we really are without all the pretenses and masks, we will find what produced *us*! God does not reside in some religious rituals. She is the makeup and core of our very being! That is why religion and conformity are the easy ways out! They never require us to get to the core of us!

When you get back to the center, there are no more blame games. You no longer blame your life on outside circumstances. Getting back to the center forces you to take ownership of your own life. That is where you will find the voice of God truly speaking in your life! We have given millions of dollars to prophets outside of us, who have lied and manipulated Biblical texts for their own villainous purposes.

This is the generation in which these middlemen and outside voices must be silenced, and the voice of God is eager to speak through you. When will you have the chance to take ownership of your own life and truly get back to your center? Most of us have no idea what it is that we truly enjoy, because we have been taught for so long what we can and cannot like. We have had rules and requirements placed on us in the name of God that have absolutely nothing to do with God—such as not drinking alcohol. We have had governments, society, and social media all forcing us to see ourselves delusionally.

Not being centered has forced us to navigate through life with such a negative outlook. Trust me, I know this oh so well from my own experience. I was in and out of "situationships," claiming that I had found true love, not knowing that those relationships were only temporary, filling voids that I was too immature to face and deal with on my own. Those voids were within me. That was not an outside battle. It was purely internal.

It is possible to follow principles that bring you great wealth. However, no matter what your financial success may be, you are still responsible for your internal work to evolve into something far deeper than just dreams of material riches. When you get centered, you will begin to develop a positive self-image, not just the fraudulent image or delusion of grandeur.

A positive self-image will change the way you think, believe, and behave, because it will only allow you to accept good things into your life. A positive self-image will never allow you to make a negative decision against yourself, no matter the situation or environment you are in.

CHAPTER 6

Positive Self-Images!

It's not what we say out loud that really determines our lives. It's what we whisper to ourselves that has the most power.

—Unknown

HAVING A POSITIVE self-image, which is the direct result of being free, is a concept that people today have difficulty accepting. This concept of seeing oneself positively is a secret to many, and yet it is the answer to everyone. Literally changing the way we see ourselves could change the entire course of human history and the limited perceptions we have created of the people we share this planet with.

Unfortunately, today we are acclimated to a time in human history in which we are systematically and routinely presented with false ideas of separation. Over time, we have somehow lost the brilliance of our conception that we are one with God, adopting instead an idea of self that does not serve who we are intrinsically.

Everything that we have become as a people is now defined by superficial connections. The very essence of our being is overshadowed by our settling for living life on a very low frequency. We settle for mediocrity, never believing that there is an ever living power that resides within us.

It is that power that people search for over a lifetime, but they often have no idea that they are seeking that power. The concept of separation from God is not one that I have always understood. In fact, recognizing that false concept is quite new to me. And that new knowledge has been revealed through much loss and pain. I have lived the majority of my life as if I were separated from the Source. This idea that I was separate from that power caused me to view myself in a way that diminished my value of myself.

One of the greatest ways to break the human spirit is to teach it that it is in constant conflict with the divine— that for one's entire life God is consumed in anger and wrath over the decisions one makes. It is demoralizing to be constantly taught that you are separate from the divine and from everything and everyone else.

We live in a society that is consumed with marketing ploys and strategies that always tend to reveal how deficient and lame we are without the latest gadgets and toys. Furthermore, we are distracted by a government that is obsessed with forcing us to revel in false patriotism and pride, while totally neglecting us.

Perhaps, after you've purchased the latest this and that, you're still not quite as fulfilled as you thought. And many people refuse to admit the countless years they have spent following a religious system, idea, philosophy, law, rule, or concept and still left without any real spiritual encounter. No matter how we attempt to place those religious concepts in our lives, they will all continue to leave us empty because they are not essentially designed to sustain our intrinsic value or worth.

Please don't misunderstand me. I'm not talking about just looking in a mirror and telling yourself a mantra of positive things. Nor am I against mantras that help to create the image or identity with which you choose to envision yourself. However, I am talking about actually doing the work—digging deep into yourself, and coming to know that you are brilliant by design, without religious dogma, government banter, or the latest marketing ploys telling you how much better off you would be with some new product.

Now again, I don't want to sound like I'm on some pedestal, or I'm some kind of guru who has it all together. On the contrary, I had to experience profound negativity in my life to get me to this understanding. Some lessons you just have to learn through losing. I had to learn the power of positive self-images by experiencing the power of negative ones. And trust me, it was no laughing matter.

For some individuals, the thought of having positive self-images may sound like a marketing ploy or an empty promise that if you follow certain steps, your whole life will turn around. And people trapped in a fundamental religious background may view the concept of positive self-images as just some kind of "New Age" baloney—a twisted and distorted way to view scripture. And that's cool! Trust me, I get it. But nothing could be further from the truth.

I have no steps for you to follow. Nor am I advocating a New Age thought to distort the way you should see God. If anything, positive self-images are a simple reminder of who you truly are. Just think of this for a moment: Why do we think it's okay to harbor so many negative ideas about ourselves? Just think for a moment of a negative situation you've found yourself in at some point in life. How did that negative situation make you feel? You can almost tangibly sense the vibration of that negative energy and the signals it sent throughout your body. Negative situations can literally have negative effects on your body, in the same way that positivity can have miraculous effects on your body.

I was taught in religious institutions that I had to hate myself, and never see myself as worthy or enough! That was a heavy burden to carry around. Seeing myself as God sees me shifted that negative dogma into a vibrant life filled with Love.

I know that I'm more than enough, because I'm made in God's image and likeness. I am divine by nature and not by default. I don't have to work at it. I simply have to *be* it! Remember, I said that positive self-images will cause you to change the way you think, believe, and behave. When you change the way you think about yourself in the light of God's Love, that changes any beliefs and dogmas that don't serve your higher self.

> *"For I know the thoughts that I think towards you," says Yahweh, "thoughts of peace, and not of evil, to give you hope and a future."* (Jeremiah 29:11)

> *"Beloved, I pray that in all respects you may prosper and be in good health, just as your soul prospers."* (3 John 1:2)

These are Old and New Testament promises from Yahweh concerning us. Yet, these promises pale in comparison to what the institutions in our lives depict. That's because those institutions were never designed to give you an identity. In fact, they do the total opposite. They rob you of identity, creativity, and individuality. They dub you into a carbon copy of what they think you should be, only allowing you to push the limits so far.

Positive self-images promote maturity and evolution. But they require responsibility, which is why so many people choose conformity. Some individuals are simply afraid of what they would be if they were totally free. But if you learn to live from unconditional Love, positive self-images are really pretty simple. However, you must first learn unconditional Love for *yourself.* You cannot do that if your dogma continuously rehearses in your mind that you are unworthy. That's just simply impossible! You cannot hold a negative thought and simultaneously have a positive experience. The thought or belief will match the experience every single time. Religion is a failed attempt at trying to create spiritual identity.

> *"You're hopeless, you religion scholars and Pharisees! Frauds! You burnish the surface of your cups and bowls so they sparkle in the sun, while the insides are maggoty with your greed and gluttony. Stupid Pharisee! Scour the insides, and then the gleaming surface will mean something.*
>
> *"You're hopeless, you religion scholars and Pharisees! Frauds! You're like manicured grave plots, grass clipped and the flowers bright, but six feet down it's all rotting bones and worm-eaten flesh. People look at you and think you're saints, but beneath the skin you're total frauds.*
>
> *"You're hopeless, you religion scholars and Pharisees! Frauds! You build granite tombs for your prophets and marble monuments for your saints."* (Matthew 23:26-28)

This is literally a definition of modern-day Christianity—and many other religious sects around the world. It is even a great reflection of government institutions. Everyone in this so called kingdom is so concerned with images that they neglect the real work.

I am literally watching family members die a slow death in misery, all for the sake of image and conformity, which keep them from ever experiencing real life. So long as they can get one of those granite tombs and be called "generals in the kingdom," they are willing to live out their final years in dead churches, instead of natural, organic, free-flowing relationships.

Positive self-images would correct all of that in an instant, helping you to realize that you are more than enough and more than deserving. Yet, you will never truly get to experience positive self-images until you accept the damage that you have caused to yourself and others.

I have watched too many people die at very young ages, never even getting half a chance to live. They were cut down short by the lies that the fundamentalist religions continue to ignore, instead demonizing and spewing rhetoric against everything they refuse to understand.

Matthew tells us that none of that fluff and stuff even matters if the real business of Love is neglected. We have adopted fraudulent relationships with fake fellow church members, while demonizing blood family members for being real by not believing the way fundamentalist religions choose to believe.

Matthew gives a clear depiction of today's culture— how we choose images over reality and then sit in misery when they yield no fruit. And I mean this in every area and aspect of our lives. When we see these false images of love and relationships, we desire those things for the sake of having the images.

"People call you saints and underneath you are total frauds." Positive self-images resolve this issue, because when we start to see ourselves as God sees us, our affections begin to change. Positive self-images are at the core of true freedom. That is why they are not readily accepted by many people. Individuals who are not secure in their own image will always feel the need to correct and change the images of others. They never get to fully experience those others by the "spirit" because they are consistently forced and self-condemned to judge solely after the flesh.

> *Oh yes, you shaped me first inside, then out; you formed me in my mother's womb. I thank you, High God—you're breathtaking! Body and soul, I am marvelously made! I worship in adoration—what a creation! You know me inside and out, you know every bone in my body; You know exactly how I was made, bit by bit, how I was sculpted from nothing into something. Like an open book, you watched*

> *me grow from conception to birth; all the stages of my life were spread out before you, The days of my life all prepared, before I'd even lived one day.* (Psalms 139:13-16)

Isn't David's praise to God in this Psalm great? Look at how he expresses his gratitude to the Most High for his own being. This is what Positive Self-Images will produce when they are fully experienced. Gratitude begins to fill every cell of your being for your divinity.

David says the greatness of this design is the fact that God knows us inside and out, including every bone in our bodies. This idea is powerful because it means that nothing about us is hidden from God. That is what should fortify our identity in Him!

From the moment we are conceived, our entire lives are spread out before Him like an open book! There is no need for fear, guilt, or shame, because all the days of our lives were prepared before we lived one day! David did not worship in adoration merely at how breathtaking God is. He realized that God proved His magnificence in His very design.

This magnificence is what true worship and adoration will bring about when one walks in positive self-images, which recognize our duality and our right to choose to operate from that duality. Hopefully, we will choose to only operate in a manner that will bring about positive results in our own lives, never needing to lord our beliefs, opinions, or doctrines over others.

You must only see the good in your brothers and sisters and continuously reinforce that good until they are able to see it in themselves. The quotations that I've used to start these chapters are more than just fancy quotes to prove my heightened sense of intelligence. If they are really absorbed, they are brief moments of clarity with profound insights. As I close this chapter, let us briefly look at the quote that Spirit inspired for this chapter:

> *It's not what we say out loud that really determines our lives. It's what we whisper to ourselves that has the most power.*
>
> —Unknown

Understanding the weight of this clarity could literally change the trajectory of our lives. We spend a lifetime keeping up with the images that we portray to the outside world, while the internal chatter that we speak is eating us alive from the inside out. These negative guarded excuses that we have created for our lives and continue to reinforce through bad theology are stifling our communities from welcoming all the infinite expressions of God's design that are needed to bring about revolutionary change to a stagnant and destitute people.

Positive self-images will immediately begin to repair the damage we have allowed to fester, because once we start to see ourselves as worthy and more than enough, those positive self-images immediately begin to shift the universe in response to the new way we see ourselves. We owe it to ourselves and our children to change any pathology that does not allow for positive self-images— not to mention that it is well past time for a new way of thinking, believing, and behaving!

Chapter 7

Jesus Freaks!

*Those Jesus Freaks, well, they're friendly, but the
shit they believe has got their minds all shut.*
                                        —Frank Zappa

Without a shadow of a doubt, it is safe to
assume that we have viewed the first man,
Adam, incorrectly. It is definitely also safe to assume that
we have clearly mistaken the purpose of the last Adam—
that is, Jesus. Many of you, who are learned in the true
history of Jesus and His life, may already know that *Jesus*
is a man-made name, for there was no letter *J* in Hebrew
or in Greek during Biblical times. In Hebrew, His name
is Yeshua.

Cool! I am very glad that you're aware of that! But, in a culture in which we have coined the phrase *Jesus Freaks*, please allow me to walk just a bit slowly for those for whom this message may come as a surprise. Many people have heard me talk about Jesus, and I have made it very clear that Christians have had an unhealthy relationship with Him. In fact, on some levels, we have created a psychologically abusive relationship with Him. And now we can hopefully see by our deficient understanding of Adam that we have been misled. We have turned Jesus into a marketing strategy for the broken, the broke, the disillusioned, and all the other people who feel that their lives are spiraling out of control.

We have used fear and the idea of separation from divinity and each other—as a result of our "fall" in consciousness in the Garden of Eden—to brutally whip so many, destroying countless families in the process. We have even used Jesus to teach hatred and racism. Never forget that the Ku Klux Klan began as a Christian organization—burning crosses on people's lawns!

For centuries, we have watched countless religious wars, without either side ever getting to the fundamental teaching of its own religious practice—which is LOVE! And that will always happen, because the fundamental practice of religions is to teach their followers to defend their beliefs—even in the face of all the lies about those beliefs and their leaders being exposed as thieves and conmen.

For more than thirty years, I defended my religious doctrines and dogmas, even when they were hurting me the most. Many people have dismissed my arguments about religion, stating that I only want to teach love because I need something to cover up my homosexuality. And they say this with such assurance, as if they know me and have walked in my shoes. Assuming that one knows the truth of another's experience is part of the delusional practice of human beings, for if those people actually knew me, they would know that their argument is totally false.

When I was younger and in the height of what some would call my "praise and worship phase," I would get done doing praise and worship in the church where my stepfather was the minister, step outside, and watch the people walking by. That was in the heart of Brownsville, Brooklyn, in the early 1990s—which were a different time and place. As I watched those people, something truly disturbed me and led me to a thought—a thought that's probably the very reason I have written this book.

I had been taught that those passersby were outsiders—despicable people who did despicable things.

Unless they adopted my concept of the relationship with God, they were going straight to Hell!

That bothered me for a very long time, because I needed the answer to why. *Why* were they going to Hell, since I knew for a fact that the members of my own church were even more sinful than they were—starting with my stepfather. But we'll get to that later.

The truth is that I asked that question long before I even began to deal with my own sexual nature. And I needed a real answer, not just some religious dance around the issue—something that would literally shift the trajectory of my life.

The warped understanding of God that was followed in my church allowed for just the right amount of fear. That fear permitted the religious leaders to dominate my relationship with God, the sacred and divine.

We need to see just how damaging allowing the interpretations of others to dictate our lives and experiences can be. Those interpretations allow for all types of prejudices, hatred, intolerance, and injustice.

By now, the reader should see how damaging it can be when the thoughts and opinions of others affect how we see ourselves. That is the most damaging kind of destruction, because we project how we feel about ourselves out into the world. If that view of ourselves is negative, that can be totally self-destructive and even deadly—especially when scripture is manipulatively used to support that negative self-image. In that case, fear has so gripped our understanding that we will not even allow any new thoughts or ideas to enter our minds. That fear teaches us that we are never to think outside the box of the scriptures as they have been taught to us.

At this point, I should clarify the difference between context and pretext:

Context (noun): "the words that are used with a certain word or phrase and that help to explain its meaning." (Merriam-Webster)

Pretext (noun): "a reason that you give to hide your real reason for doing something." (Merriam-Webster)

Notice how context has no hidden motives. It seeks only to make clear or to explain the meaning of what is being said. Pretext, on the other hand, has hidden motives. When we take Biblical text out of context, we create pretext—a motive that hides the truest intent of the text.

The moment we take Biblical text out of context, it not only loses its purpose, but it also loses its power. That's why we have so many powerless religious robots stuck in stagnation and conformity, masquerading around as if they have reached the depths of the mysteries of God.

Those robots are not even aware that they are lost in the nonsense of old men's fables and traditions. This aimless wandering is devastating our communities, because conformity gives us scapegoats that permit us to refuse to take responsibility for our own actions.

When we are religiously intolerant, we literally have the nerve to get arrogantly aggressive in our error and even expect the wrath of God to support us in it. Religion and society have literally created a platform for the ignorant to perform without any real viable message to bring about true freedom in the life of God's people.

Real truth does not need the assistance of charismatic delivery. Truth is powerful in and of itself, and should not merely be felt, but also cognitively understood and shared practically, so that it induces real change in the lives of those who hear and receive it. Unfortunately, many people have allowed society to dumb them down to such a level that they may even find it offensive to be challenged to think.

As I have said before, all of my trouble with religion started the moment I began to think for myself. That's when I was able to speak about the physical and verbal abuse being done to me, because intelligence and intellect are almost totally forbidden in today's religious culture.

When people dumb down their relationship with God, they place the burden on the awakened and the strong to carry the weight of our culture. However, they simultaneously devalue and underappreciate those people, while celebrating and honoring those who seek to rob, steal, and take from everyone. Awakened and strong people are what the Bible refers to as the "remnant"—the very few who refuse to bow to the fake and fraudulent systems of this world. These very few strong people know that their identity is not developed from the outside, but from the inside, which takes a lifetime of discipline and commitment.

Much of the pretext that we have accepted as truth is literally killing us. Yet, hearing the freedom that comes with context scares the hell out of us! And the lies create a convenient space for us to hide, even if that space is uncomfortable. Pretext allows us to say that we love others without ever truly having to live up to that promise. Pretext becomes our guarded excuse to live contrary to our original purpose and design.

Furthermore, pretext allows us to label people and treat them based on the lies we've been taught about them. If we continue in this judgmental, condemning, narcissistic way, we are going to destroy each other before long. Lies have controlled the way we've been forced to see ourselves and others. We've clearly seen, within our short generation, just how destructive dogmatic religious and governmental control can be. However, we are living in a generation that will break and destroy these dogmatic pretexts—and not just merely as an act of rebellion or defiance!

Now, don't get me wrong. There was a period in my life during which I was a poster child for the Jesus Freaks. In fact, I carried that label with honor and distinction, because I thought it was my obligation as a Christian. I thought at that time that I was consumed with love and devotion for God.

Being a Jesus Freak meant that I was to obey Jesus' teachings, be a part of a Bible-believing church, stand on the "word of God," obey my leaders, spread the Gospel, and try to get more and more people into our churches!

Oddly, most Christians today would agree that those are noble things that we should be doing. We owe God that much. But let's be honest. That's a far cry from what we actually do. We are so far removed from being like Christ that "Jesus Freak" isn't even a compliment in today's vernacular, because there are so many Jesus Freaks who cause so much tension, hatred, intolerance, prejudice, envy, and jealousy in the world. Trust me, the negative list goes on and on.

Please, let me say, I in no way want to make my readers feel like they are the lowest of the low as Bible thumpers or religious fanatics, who are worthy of death. But the pretext that we have adopted as truth has made the behaviors of the so-called saints unbearable.

Because I grew up in the church, I know firsthand the negative behaviors that religiously controlled minds can produce by taking Biblical texts out of context. A massive nucleus of unlearned religious leaders have taught us to be in constant conflict with the world and everything in it.

Once again, fear of believing anything outside of what you have been taught may make it difficult for you to accept the truth, even when you finally hear it in context. When I realized how simple the Gospel of Jesus truly is, I was in shock. It took me a while to grasp that I had spent most of my life teaching and preaching lies!

I entitled this chapter "Jesus Freaks" because I wanted to make clear that it was Jesus Freaks like my former self who spend a lifetime dedicated to the service of the church, or what they now call the "kingdom," without ever knowing the true Gospel of Jesus Christ! So many Jesus Freaks have no idea what the Gospel is. The church or organized religion have left out the very essence of the

Gospel—that is, the "good news"! Organized religion has become all ritual and rule with *no* Good News!

CHAPTER 8

"For God So Loved the World!"

*God is Love. Therefore Love. Without distinc-
tion, without calculation, without procrastina-
tion, Love.*

—Henry Drummond

Now that Spirit has allowed me to go through the rant of the previous chapter, we can get a clearer understanding of the message and love of Jesus Christ. As I said at the beginning of this book, I am not trying to force anyone to believe in Jesus. Nor am I trying to create a new doctrine surrounding Him. I do, however, want to show my readers just how clear and simple Christ's message truly is. It's so simple that most people will condemn it as heresy and call it the height of sacrilege, not even realizing that love is at the very center of it.

Trust me, it was devastating for me to get this level of clarity, to see just how wrong I had God and His love toward us. The moment I applied logic and reason to the narrative of Jesus' Biblical life, the Gospel seemed almost too good to be true.

Even today, when many religious leaders hear my newfound insights, they immediately proclaim that I am guilty of trying to make the Gospel too simple. That has always struck me as odd, because they appear to be arguing that the Gospel should be tedious and complex. Only someone who is truly Antichrist would make the Gospel inaccessible to everyone, right? But let's not get into another rant. Instead, let's see if we can apply a little bit of logic and reason to the life of Christ and simplify what others have made difficult.

There are holidays that celebrate the life of Jesus. One of the most popular of those holidays, with Jesus at the center, is Christmas. People have debated whether we should say "Merry Christmas" or "Happy Holidays." The latter upsets the Jesus Freaks because they believe it takes Christ out of Christmas!

But to turn to the subject of this chapter, let us look at the following quotation:

> *For God so loved the world, that he gave his only begotten Son, that whosoever believeth in him should not perish, but have everlasting life.* (John 3:16)

This Biblical verse is probably not only the first one many of us learned as children, but also the central theme and concept of the entire New Testament. As children, we probably didn't understand the major impact this verse had on our lives, because it was just a cute little verse to quote on Children's Day.

In fact, this one verse is more important than anything else Jesus did on Planet Earth! It is actually the reason for *everything* He did while He was here.

The lack of understanding by religious leaders concerning this verse has caused a tremendous amount of devastation on our planet. This verse is more important than the ones describing the Angel appearing to Mary. It is more important than the verses about the death, burial, and resurrection of Jesus. I know that many readers will think that's crazy, but it's true. It is the one verse that we should never let out of our sight or understanding.

When this verse is fully understood, that can begin to drastically change the course of human history! Let's take it piece by piece and see if we can get clarity from it and begin to throw off some of the chains that have held us in bondage.

"For God so *loved the world*"! Damn! That is so powerful to me! The entire understanding of Christ starts right here in these few short words. No Biblical debate matters, no doctrinal feuds need to continue. The foundation for "everything Jesus" starts right here!

"For God so loved the world, that *he gave his only begotten Son.*" Now we get to see this together for what it is truly worth. Most people will get excited over the fact that the Son was *given*; hence, the reason why Jesus has become so commercialized and yet never truly experienced.

And we leave out the "For God so loved the world" part. Here is why that part is the most important aspect of our fundamental understanding of Christ: It was love that sent Jesus here. He was sent out of love! Somehow, many of us have forgotten that simple truth.

If we are to truly believe that God so loved the World that He would give His Son, then we must also assume that love is God's greatest intention for us! That's not merely my excuse for being a proud homosexual! This verse confirms that love is the supreme motive and intention, and perhaps that is why such a simple profound truth has gone ignored for so long!

For centuries, we have lived under the diabolical notion that God is angry at us and that we deserve nothing but death. We still teach today how God's wrath, jealousy, anger, and disdain for everyone and everything that isn't Christian is waiting for us right around the corner.

This message pales drastically in comparison to the purpose for which God gave us his Son. How is it that, according to today's church and religious Bible thumpers, God is villainously angry and seeks nothing but revenge for wretched man?

Why is it so strange for us to believe that God truly loves the world and everyone in it? I'm sure it's because of Adam's fall in consciousness, which created a delusional God image, and in turn a delusional self-image.

According to this very simple verse in John, it must become clear to us that by picturing God as intolerant, we are denying the message of this verse—which is that God loves us. If we ignore the powerful words *for God so loved the world*, we also change the purpose and power of Jesus Christ. In fact, we actually annihilate the Gospel if we remove those few words.

I know that we have been taught that the Gospel is principally about the death, burial, and resurrection of Jesus, and that sounds great in a charismatic church sermon. But it's not true! The Gospel is not about Jesus' death; the Gospel is about His birth!

For countless years, we have misunderstood the true meaning of the Gospel, and that has caused countless misconceptions and fraudulent spiritual lives. The real Gospel is about God loving the world! There would be no virgin birth that could lead to Calvary Hill if not *for God so loved the world*!

Having an unclear understanding of God's posture toward the world tends to lead people to speak on His behalf in ways that they should not. We have become a generation that is trying to break down and grasp the depths of the mysteries of Christ. And we had no idea that His greatest mystery lay in *for God so loved the world*!

Those few words are the reason we have a New Testament in the first place. Yet, most of our churches and religious institutions have made those words of little or no consequence. Not knowing God's posture and heart toward the world is the very thing that has led to messages of condemnation and religious and spiritual abuse.

I cannot even begin to remember how many sermons I have lived through and even preached myself in which nothing but hatred and anger came across—a hatred and anger that stemmed from an understanding that God is an angry old man, who judges and condemns the world, and everyone and everything that isn't like Him—with homosexuals at the top of the list. How did we get to such a view of God, which has truly led to a misunderstanding and miscalculation of Jesus' purpose?

By creating pretext, we have become anti the very thing we claim to love the most. And our blind devotion has only prevented us from seeing truth as we should. Simply keeping *for God so loved the world* at the center of our understanding would have caused us to live from that knowledge. And we would have created a better world for ourselves—one in which we "walk not after the flesh, but after the spirit" (Romans 8:1).

"For God so *loved* the world" is the entire reason and purpose for the life and ministry of Jesus Christ. This hasn't changed because we have found shrewd marketing strategies to win people over to our delusion through fear. My real question is, what happened to our understanding of God loving the world?

How do we have so many doctrines, sermons, and teachings about Jesus and never hear this foundational truth that God loves the world? Knowing "For God so *loved* the world" as a principle would have kept us in line with His message! And that certainly would have served as a reminder to His purpose!

By not keeping this simple yet powerful truth in our understanding, we have not only alienated so many people from the message of Christ, but we have alienated ourselves from the fullness of His message and His love.

Even if everything about Jesus that came after John 3:16 were lies and plagiarism, this truth that "For God so *loved* the world that He gave us His Son" would have at least afforded us the knowledge that His purpose and reason for coming was out of love, and not from a vindictive hatred toward mankind.

The loving New Testament depiction of God's posture toward mankind tells us that "For God so loved the world that He gave us His Son!" And if God's posture toward us is love, who is the source of condemnation?

CHAPTER 9

No Condemnation!

*Any fool can criticize, complain, and condemn—
and most fools do. But it takes character and
self-control to be understanding and forgiving.*
—Dale Carnegie

I CAN ALMOST HEAR the religious backlash from this chapter of *Freedom, the New Heresy!* Because it's at the core of why freedom has been brandished as heresy and total abandonment of God's values. And that couldn't be further from the truth.

So many people are going to warn against this type of teaching and call it propaganda, claiming it's just a twisting of scriptures for my own personal gain and benefit, because a homosexual has to use every scripture on love to justify his or her lifestyle. I want to take that ignorance down a notch.

The most promiscuous time in my life occurred while I was serving in church as a teenager, going through all the fake motions, pretending to be righteous, while I used midnight musicals to see whom I might conquer next sexually. But I never needed justification when I kept my lifestyle secret. So, surely you can't seriously believe that when I'm in my forties, I somehow need justification. I don't!

At some point, we all have to grow up, evolve, and mature from a primitive understanding of God through Christ Consciousness, or the survival of our species may be beyond repair! Not to mention that we should not be in the Information Age and not have real, viable spiritual information—that is, information that liberates us and sets us free! For religion is the preaching of freedom, but the practice of bondage.

The members of this generation are not trying to be disrespectful to the aged, but they are demanding their right to be free! The primitive understanding of God that consumed our lives through rituals, services, and mundane sacrifice is rapidly coming to a close, even if we choose to ignore it and blame it on rebellion and people leaving God.

While the new understanding of God is true, it's an act of rebellion—but a necessary rebellion! You see, the weight of religion has become unbearable to this generation, and to tell the truth, it's been burdensome for decades now. It's a burden that so many are refusing to carry anymore.

It's a weight to have someone standing over you, constantly telling you that you are not enough! You're too this, and you're too that! And that's especially when you begin to take on those false religious ideas as truth and carry that weight and burden into your reality.

I want to make clear that this new understanding of God has nothing to do with people leaving God. Do not make the mistake of assuming that because people are falling away from religious ideology, they are leaving God. On the contrary, they are leaving behind a primitive understanding of God for one that serves their higher self.

And I might add, it's a journey that you, dear reader, should embark upon, too. Otherwise, sooner rather than later, you will realize that your religious devotion may end up leaving you empty.

> *For God sent not his Son into the world*
> *to condemn the world; but that the world*
> *through him might be saved.* (John 3:17)

This is another truth about Jesus that we use to close out sermons to get an emotional response. However, its full potential and power are never fully experienced or understood.

The verse just before this one, John 3:16, tells us that God sent His Son because he so loved the world. So, now we clearly understand that the Son's purpose was (and is) love. However, in John 3:17, God wants us to be clear about what he did *not* send Jesus to do: "For God sent not his Son into the world to condemn the world."

Do you get how powerful this message is? As I read this verse, it almost sounds like a warning that no matter what man-made religious systems of this world may say, Jesus' purpose was *never* to condemn! And that's not because Jesus was so righteous either, but because God never intended Him for that mission. How is it that we live in a culture that has nothing but condemnation to offer in the name of Jesus?

Once again, God *never* put condemnation in Jesus' mission statement. I was taught to preach condemnation as a part of my holiness message, yet it was never intended in the purpose of Christ. Now that you are beginning to see the truth, I hope you see that the real message of Christ has been obscured by the message of organized religion.

Jesus intended to liberate; religion intends to enslave! That is why the concept of condemnation is so valuable to organized religion. If the religious leaders can get you to believe that you are condemned, they can control you with fear—using that fear to market their solution to the Adam problem: Original Sin!

Why did God want us to know, even before He sent his Son, that Jesus was not sent to condemn humanity? Could it be that He knew there were people who would distort Jesus' mission for their own benefit? The very idea of condemnation creates an environment for guilt and shame, because people have to believe that they have standards to measure up to. Look at what the word *condemn* actually means:

> *condemn* (verb): to say in a strong and definite way that someone or something is bad or wrong; to give (someone) a usually severe punishment; to cause (someone) to suffer or live in difficult or unpleasant conditions. (Merriam-Webster)

I am so thankful to The Most High, because even when Adam fell in consciousness and forgot who he was, God never forgot who *we* were! And because "God so loved the world," the very definition and essence of condemnation never entered into His plan for us.

Now look at this quote from scripture:

> *There is therefore now no condemnation to them which are in Christ Jesus, who walk not after the flesh, but after the spirit.* (Romans 8:1)

For decades, I believed that this quote only applied to those of us in the church, "the kingdom," who accept Christ. But that's not true! Paul doesn't say that there is no condemnation for those who have accepted Christ. He said that persons who live in Christ Consciousness possess no condemnation.

Such individuals possess no condemnation because they are awakened—that is, made aware that condemnation was never in Jesus' mission. Romans 8:1 does not merely mean that individuals are not condemned. On the contrary! It is saying that individuals who are truly in Christ Jesus do not live in, with, or through condemnation.

Paul even gives you the reason why individuals who live in Christ Consciousness do not possess condemnation—namely, "they walk not after the flesh, but after the spirit." Individuals who live in Christ Consciousness do not judge the flesh. They judge or live from the vibration and frequency of spirit!

Condemnation is the product of man's fall or shift in consciousness or awareness. It is not a part of our original design. Don't forget, Adam and Eve were already "naked and not ashamed." What changed? Their nakedness was not merely about their physical bodies. It meant that they were not hiding anything from God.

Everything about their relationship was out in the open. They were the ones who saw the need to dress and cover what was already seen by God. Yet, I always find it strange that Jesus, the spotless lamb according to religious teachings, did not come into the world to condemn it. On the other hand, there's always Aunt Mary Righteousness and Big Uncle William Judgmental who feel that it's their job to condemn.

"There is…no condemnation" does not create a New Age right for a free-for-all, so that people can do whatever they want. Condemnation robs people of true and authentic freedom to be who God made them to be! Period!

When I gave my life to religious control and man-made doctrines and ideologies, I suffered because I felt that I was continuously in conflict with God. Religion is not an environment that can produce a healthy relationship with the divine.

I said earlier that, as we continue this discussion, the Gospel would almost seem too good to be true—not because it's difficult to believe, but because religion has made it so impossible to accept. In our imagination, it is difficult for us to accept that there are no strenuous requirements to be in fellowship with God. As I have already said, I have been tried in the courts of religious hierarchy, which have found me guilty of making God too convenient. But what father would make himself inconvenient or inaccessible to his children? Somehow the God of religion has become that father—inconvenient and inaccessible to his children.

Knowing that God has no intention to condemn me allows me the freedom to love myself and see myself as I should, without fear or condemnation. I am now able to experience life and the people in the world as I should, knowing that my experience does not offend God!

Many Jesus Freaks boast about how faithful they have been to their religion. But they have only gained bragging rights about their successes within their own

FREEDOM THE NEW HERESY

religious communities, having very little impact on the world around them. They are drowning in the belief that God requires so much of them. And oddly, the payment for all of their work and religious grinding is not even received in life. It's a victory they believe they only receive in Heaven. Meanwhile, others who do not subscribe to such nonsensical practices live an abundant life here on Earth.

Simply by knowing that there is no condemnation, these liberated people are able to destroy the labels that religion and society have ignorantly placed on others. Condemnation and incorrect judgment can cause you to miss your next opportunity.

Feeding off damnation and condemnation, religious and governmental institutions control how people navigate through society. They create the police, who make sure that everyone keeps up with this fraudulent moral code—a code that works for some, while damning and condemning others.

This is not even a religious issue! People who may not even value Biblical texts have come to realize, if only through common sense, that condemnation and judging do not work and only bring about adverse effects.

> *...but that the world through him might be saved.* (John 3:17)

In this generation, we are being awakened to the real Gospel of Jesus Christ, which started before Jesus even arrived on the scene. The Gospel did not begin on Christmas Day. The Gospel, or "good news," started with God and His posture of love toward humanity, which led to His Son.

The loving Father laid a clear foundation and purpose for His Son regarding mankind, and that purpose was *love*! Jesus did not come to tell people how horrific they were or to level them with wrath and judgment. There is no condemnation in Jesus. and the latter part of John 3:17 explains why:

That the world through him might be saved.

Let's look at the meaning of the word *save*:

> *Save*: (verb): to keep (someone or something) safe; to stop (someone or something) from dying or being hurt, damaged, or lost; to stop (something) from ending or failing; to make something that is in danger of failing

successful; to keep something from being lost
or wasted. (Merriam-Webster)

This is "good news" because it is the real Gospel of
Jesus Christ! Condemnation was not His purpose. Man's
fall in consciousness had already perverted him with such
a notion. Jesus came to restore our awareness that there is
no condemnation.

CHAPTER 10

The Unlikely Source of Condemnation

We cannot change anything until we accept it.
Condemnation does not liberate, it oppresses.

—Carl Jung

I MUST BE HONEST. As I sat to write this chapter, I already knew what the Spirit would have me say. Even during the months that I had writer's block and couldn't pen these thoughts, I knew this chapter was coming. And now that I have actually written the chapter, it is hitting me in a different way.

I recognize the gravity of going against the grain by having a message that differs greatly from that of the system. But even as I was experiencing writer's block, I couldn't wait to add this chapter to the book.

I remember exactly how I felt when I realized where condemnation came from. Reason and intellect were forbidden in my religious community, so I can understand how the members of that community might be offended by what I have to say here. Nevertheless, I harbor no resentment or anger toward any group of people. But I must address religious communities in a way that initiates healthy discussion and brings about real change.

In the last few chapters, we discussed the real foundation of the Gospel. We learned that although we have a form of Godliness, religions totally deny that power. But Jesus' mission was "For God so loved the world!" If we are going to be followers of Christ's teachings, our mission and purpose on Earth should be love as well.

We have also learned that not only did God lay the foundation of the Gospel in love, but He also issued a clear disclaimer that Jesus' purpose was *not* to condemn the world. As I have repeatedly noted, we live in a culture in which Jesus Freaks have adopted a posture of condemnation, death, Hell, and utter destruction. It is the most religious people who have leveled on the rest of the world their disdain for God.

It is totally unfair to accuse people of wanting to live any way they wish, just because they no longer obey religion's dogmatic control. It is not the so-called world that is creating a false delusional relationship with God.

I have entitled this chapter "The Unlikely Source of Condemnation," and rightfully so, because religion has made it difficult for people to understand that condemnation was not in Jesus' mission statement. If that is so, where did all this condemnation come from? The answer is simple: Religion!

The truth is a difficult pill to swallow. "He that hath ears to hear, let him hear" (Matthew 11:15).

It is very easy for people who condemn others to ignore truth. They believe that they are the elite representatives of God, who have a monopoly to speak on His behalf. But a lie is still a lie if everyone believes it! And the truth is still the truth if no one believes it.

In this culture, if one person of influence says something, religious people will believe it as truth without ever checking it for themselves. The delusional image of man's fall in consciousness allows the lie that they have created about us to be readily accepted, while they demonize the truth and even financially support those who keep us enslaved.

But let's get back to the point at hand. We have finally reached the generation that is brilliant enough to ask the questions, "What is the source of all this condemnation? Why do we feel this incessant need to judge and demonize every aspect of human life? If Jesus truly came 'that I might have life,' how could I have that life if I'm to be in a constant state of conflict with the world?"

In order for us to discover the answer to the unlikely source of condemnation, I must take you to a discussion that Jesus had with his disciples. It's a Biblical text that most preachers ignore, but let's take a look at it for just a moment:

> Now Jesus turned to address his disciples, along with the crowd that had gathered with them: "The religion scholars and Pharisees are competent teachers in God's Law. You won't go wrong in following their teachings on Moses. But be careful about following them. They talk a good line, but they don't live it. They don't take it into their hearts and live it out in their behavior. It's all spit-and-polish veneer.

"Instead of giving you God's Law as food and drink by which you can banquet on God, they package it in bundles of rules, loading you down like pack animals. They seem to take pleasure in watching you stagger under these loads, and wouldn't think of lifting a finger to help. Their lives are perpetual fashion shows, embroidered prayer shawls one day and flowery prayers the next. They Love to sit at the head table at church dinners, basking in the most prominent positions, preening in the radiance of public flattery, receiving honorary degrees, and getting called 'Doctor' and 'Reverend.'" (Matthew 23:1-7)

Whenever I quote this Biblical text, I always like to make clear that this is Jesus speaking to us, not one of the prophets or apostles. This was Jesus giving us a warning. And like every true prophet, He must oppose religious systems, false doctrines, and dogmas!

Jesus warns us against following the religious of his time. He opposes all the things that cause us to live primitive pretexts in our everyday lives, never reaching our fullest potential. We are at the precipice of human history in which religion, especially Christianity, is experiencing people heeding this same warning today.

People are leaving the churches in droves, not because of this book, but because they have discovered that religion is a shallow attempt at relating to God. Those who stay in the churches blame hypocrisy on the devil and every outside source they can think of, without ever looking inwardly at themselves.

No one can tell me that I am making this up! For thirty years, I lived out this delusional devotion to God. But Jesus addressed the religious of his day with a message that fits today's churches, especially African American churches.

Jesus' rebuke of the religious in His time is an eerily necessary rebuke of the religious of *this* time—not to mention that if Jesus had the right to warn against following the religious of his time, we have the same right today.

In Matthew 23:4, Jesus explains that the religious communities are the unlikely source of condemnation. "How?" you ask. Jesus explains that it is the religious who oppress people with bundles of rules. Wow! Jesus is making clear to us the source of all rules and regulations!

Those rules and regulations lead to messages of condemnation, damnation, and destruction. "And you won't even lift a finger," He said, "to help carry the load you place on others!" You lorded over people as the mouthpiece of God with rules that you yourselves refuse to keep and follow.

By telling us that it is the religious who are placing all of these rules and regulations on the people, Jesus reaffirms the real Gospel message that "there is therefore now no condemnation!" He is telling us even now that He is not the source of those rules.

> *Instead of Giving you God's Law as food and drink by which you can banquet on God, they package it in bundles of rules.*

You see the real Law of God is "For God so *loved* the World!" This is the law the religious want you to ignore and to avoid. The longer you avoid it and ignore it, the more you allow them to set up as religious police in your life, continuously loading you down with rules and laws that have absolutely nothing to do with the real mission and purpose of God!

How dare you religious take a posture of arrogance when Jesus leveled such a rebuke on the religious that it speaks to you today? According to Jesus, it's you, the religious, who have consumed people's lives with mundane rituals and laws. You are in no position to judge and condemn the world!

Clearly, you are in no position to drag Jesus to your side as a defense. Now that we are becoming clear about what is true and what is false, let's make clear that we now know that you religious cannot call down the wrath of the Heavens to join you in your anger and disdain toward the rest of the world. Clearly, you cannot do that. You must see yourselves in the light of truth, realizing that religion has been and is a destructive force in our world.

Within the African American community, this condemnatory concept of God has not only caused us to be set against one another, but it has allowed for a continued state of poverty, because it has forced us to believe that God's plan for us is destruction. That causes us to settle for poverty in the name of God.

We fill the churches to the brim to get our religious fix and admiration from our religious heroes, but then we leave just as spiritually empty as when we walked in. That system is only designed to give you your religious fix for one week. Then you go back the next week for another dose.

In that system, the only one who is highly favored is the pastor. The rest of us are left barren and empty, because the system was never designed to fill our spiritual space. It was set up to keep us in a continued state of reaching, but never attaining.

So, the entire pursuit of the religious is to reach the highest place within the system, because that will prove how far they have gone toward God. Meanwhile, Jesus' message still tells us that we must be cautious about following religious people.

This abusive system is not only damaging within the confines of religion, but its effects are damaging all over the world! Religious people create delusional concepts of God that don't truly exist, and they do it blindly and arrogantly in His name.

In our culture, we have literally watched someone who wrestled with his own homosexuality walk right into the Pulse Nightclub in Orlando, Florida, and assassinate 49 people, wounding 58 others. Having a negative ideology at the center of his mind prompted that man to disrupt the lives of so many others.

But many Jesus Freaks defended his actions. And others who did not defend him wept false tears for the victims. How do I know they were false tears? Because you don't say you're sorry, and then continue to practice a belief that produces men like the assassin. You confront those ideas, see them in the light of TRUTH, and you correct them.

You don't use God as your defense when you were clearly on Jesus' list of warnings. It is time for us as a culture to mature beyond this primitive understanding of God and His posture toward the world! We can progress as a people!

> *You're hopeless, you religion scholars and Pharisees! Frauds! You go halfway around the world to make a convert, but once you get him you make him into a replica of yourselves, double damned.* (Matthew 23:14)

This is Jesus telling us that the religious are the frauds. They go around the world to gain converts, only to turn them into themselves! They are liars, thieves, closet homosexuals, rapists, abusers, cheaters, and so on. Pure frauds! But they literally spend countless millions of dollars claiming to win souls for God, while robbing people of their true identities. To me, that is one of the most grievous offenses, because religious converts may never get to truly experience who they are in God, since they have become replicas of frauds.

The millions of dollars that the religious spend, claiming to win souls, could have developed some small nations, could have developed our schools, and could have paid our teachers a fair wage.

It is clearly time for this generation to find new spiritual mentors and true teachers about the relationship with the divine. We have allowed this dumbed down version of the relationship with God because it has made us complacent about our lack of responsibility.

The truth I teach about Christ Awareness or Consciousness requires you to put in work. In these few chapters alone, if I've done nothing else, I've challenged you to grow in your understanding.

The truth does not change because you have made heroes out of liars. You have thrown Jesus in people's faces, using Him as your defense to control and dictate others' lives, while you yourselves live secret lives.

Jesus warned us against religious people, and that warning resonates throughout the ages. In the African American community, we have allowed religious misinterpretations of scripture to dominate our lives for way too long.

Fully wrapping themselves in delusional ideologies, the religious have leveled the world with false accusations that were never in the Gospel's mission statement, and they have alienated so many people from truly experiencing God.

CHAPTER 11

We Have One Father!

One father is worth more than a hundred schoolmasters.

—George Herbert

WE HAVE BECOME a primitive culture in our understanding of God as that understanding relates to Christ Consciousness, because our religious ideologies have evolved from the fall in Adam's consciousness.

This delusional way caused man to see himself as separate from God. It was that same separation that made the people say, "We need a King!" They cried this because in their delusion they didn't believe they could govern themselves. They believed that they needed someone to tell them exactly what to do.

This dumbed down version of God has required us to always need someone to lead and dictate our lives, creating the false belief that we don't possess the ability to lead ourselves in what is best for us as we navigate through life's experiences.

We allow religious leaders, politicians, teachers, social media, the news, and others to dictate how we perceive the world, never creating an identity for ourselves that serves our best interests. That's our cry. "Give me a King!"

We want something or someone that will give us identity—someone that will reinforce our weaknesses and our low self-esteem.

In Matthew 23, Jesus warns against fraudulent religious leaders, who take on title after title, promoting themselves over the people. In our ignorance, we have celebrated this as devotion to God and promotion from God.

We have used these fraudulent promotions as measuring sticks for how close someone is to God. The scripture could not speak more clearly against a culture that has adopted this false teaching of spiritual fathers. Because we have been taught to defend these fake leaders, we have excused the victimizers continuing spiritual abuse.

The victimizers have not only abused a particular group of people or members of their own religious congregations. No, it's worse than that. We have allowed them to abuse the whole community. This antiquated religious system promotes separation and division.

We all know that Christ didn't come to divide, but to bring us all together. Within the confines of genuine and organic relationship, there can be no hierarchy. False religious men and women were never intended to take a place in your life as spiritual fathers and mothers.

Hierarchy in the relationship with God creates separation, forcing people to see other people in ways that they shouldn't. Jesus said we were not to set up "experts" over our lives, who tell us what we can and cannot do. Yet, that is precisely what we have allowed our religious organizations to do. We have allowed people who claim to speak for God to control and dictate our lives. While we may celebrate that as devotion, Jesus strongly rebuked it. That position is the height of hypocrisy, and yet we claim it to be Christlike.

In our religious institutions, we have been taught that a controlling authority has been ordained by God—and not only ordained, but required to keep people in line with what God wants. Many people defend this as if it were sound Biblical teaching, when in fact it is nothing but a diabolical lie and a blatant impediment to a true organic relationship with God.

By setting up "experts" over your life, who have authority over you, you are limiting your experience to their interpretations of your life. Thus, you are no longer in control of making cognitive decisions for yourself. Not only does a manipulated and warped concept of the relationship with God rob you of authentic experience, but it also creates and promotes separation by placing the "experts" above and you below. That relationship contradicts the relationship Christ intended us to have with one another. He describes that true relationship in the same verse….

> *You all have a single Teacher, and you are all classmates.* (Matthew 23:8)

Jesus placed us all on the same level. We are all classmates, needing to learn some of the same lessons. Real leaders don't lead by robbing others of their identity. Real leaders return identities that have been stolen or manipulated. Conformity has become the easy way out for so many, especially in the African American religious and secular communities.

That is why we use the Bible to demonize the many forms of black creativity and individuality that God chooses to express Himself, and we only regard people who look and dress like us as authentic reflections of God on Earth. That conformity gives us a crutch so that we never grow and mature in our understanding of infinite expression!

Fraudulent relationships blind us from seeing God moving in every way, especially through us. We sit in our churches and tell God that He is free to move in us, but those moves have to be verified through so-called spiritual fathers and mothers. That creates a direct hindrance to a natural, organic, and free flow of God in our lives.

As a young pastor, I only wanted what was best for the people. I begged God to flow freely in me, not realizing that in order for that free flow to truly happen, I had to be free myself. I couldn't just use words like *free* or *freedom* esoterically and never experience them fully!

That is the epitome of having "the form of Godliness and denying its power!" (II Timothy 3:5). We have begged God to do new things, while we practice and believe the same old way. And religious leaders are at the forefront of taking their followers in these religious circles, spouting dry regurgitated sermon after sermon, without ever teaching a true spiritual discipline that empowers their people to see themselves as they truly are, enabling them to take their rightful places in the world. From those "sacred pulpits," we have heard villainous messages of hatred, separation, exclusion, and intolerance, all in the name of God.

Yet, we seldom if ever hear just how much "God so loved the world." It is the message of hatred that we have adopted as a culture that has kept us in Hell:

> *Your lives are roadblocks to God's Kingdom.*
> *You refuse to enter, and won't let anyone else*
> *in either."* (Matthew 23:13)

Jesus is still lecturing the religious here, clearly showing them, and us, the difference between His message and theirs. He was clearly showing us that His message, posture, and purpose for the world would never change. He was still holding true to the Gospel message that "God did not send His Son into the world to condemn the world" (John 3:17).

The condemnatory message that we have adopted as a culture, together with the religious law enforcers that we have placed over our lives—bishops, pastors, reverends, doctors, etc.—have only served to rob people of a true and organic relationship with God. Those law enforcers have become roadblocks to people being able to see God as they should.

The message those enforcers have leveled the world with has caused a great divide in the way we see one another, creating rules and regulations that never had anything to do with God. Those rules and regulations have encapsulated our understanding of how infinitely God chooses to express Himself on Earth.

We have stagnated as a culture and have even celebrated and built monuments to our stagnation. And we have done this in the name of God, believing that it was His desire that we judge, condemn, and abstain from the world that He loved so much. And everything that we don't truly understand, or want to get to know, is at the top of our list to demonize.

Religious leaders, with a primitive understanding of God, have never experienced the God of whom they speak. And I know many are ready to debate me on saying that, believing that the emotional experience they have on Sunday mornings is the end-all to what God has extended for our lives. Those leaders at least entertain us.

We have limited God to a feeling that stimulates our emotions, but without ever bringing about any cognitive awareness. That's because religious people say, "Move my feet, but leave my mind alone." They believe that challenging people to think and to see another side is worthy of corporal punishment.

This type of fraudulent leadership never allows the individuals they're leading to enter into all that God has for them. They only create a need in people to hear their voices.

Many of these fraudulent leaders will read Matthew 23 and twist it to justify their sensationalist need for their religious heroes. They will even claim that it is me who is twisting scriptures for my own gain. Many of them believe that I am attempting to silence the voices of the preachers, so that the devil can come in and pollute the minds of the people.

None of that is true. I am simply trying to get you to focus your attention back on God and Christ Consciousness. If that is wrong, I am happily guilty of that crime. And here's why: Let's go back to Matthew 23:

> *Save that authority for God; let him tell you what to do. No one else should carry the title of "Father"; you have one father, and he's in Heaven.* (Matthew 23:9)

This quote scares most of you because you have been taught to believe that you need preachers to direct you into God's plan for your life. You have been taught that it is religious leaders who guide you to the truth. That is how cunning the lie is. You have been subtly taught to listen to the voices of others.

Jesus said to listen to the voice of God *only*. But some people believe that God cannot use any source or method that He chooses, but needs preachers to interpret Him. That was the delusional awareness of first man Adam, who started to get his information from another source, and God had to ask, "Who told you that?" The truth is that God can use a sign on a bus to answer the exact questions you have asked if He chooses to speak to you in that way.

To this day, God is asking, "Who told you that? Who told you that false information about yourself?" Sadly, for many of us, it was diabolical religious leaders with hidden motives and agendas that have given us that false information. They have led us in an endless, mundane search for God through stagnant religious practices. The longer we remain ignorant of the spiritual abuse that is taking place, the longer we will settle for things in our lives that we don't deserve.

"I Am the Good Shepherd!"

Jesus told this simple story, but they had no idea what he was talking about. So he tried again. "I'll be explicit, then. I am the Gate for the sheep. All those others are up to no good—sheep stealers, every one of them. But the sheep didn't listen to them. I am the Gate. Anyone who goes through me will be cared for—will freely go in and out, and find pasture. A thief is only there to steal and kill and destroy. I came so they can have real and eternal life, more and better life than they ever dreamed of.

"I am the Good Shepherd. The Good Shepherd puts the sheep before himself, sacrifices himself if necessary. A hired man is not a real shepherd. The sheep mean nothing to him. He sees a wolf come and runs for it, leaving the sheep to be ravaged and scattered by the wolf. He's only in it for the money. The sheep don't matter to him." (John 10:6-13)

There is a verse in John 10 that we have quoted for centuries. And like most of the verses that we have quoted, we have quoted it incorrectly. Many people even get offended when I put it back into context. That is why I have included it from the Message translation for plain English, and included the verses that surround it for clarity.

Let's take a look at the verse I want us to experience and become one with in truth:

> *A thief is only there to steal and to kill and destroy. I came so they can have real and eternal life, more and better life than they ever dreamed of.* (John 10:10)

I am certain that I am not the only one who has heard this verse before. It's been screamed and hollered with all the fervor of a normal charismatic church sermon. We've heard preachers use it to depict Satan and his minions, who go around seeking people to consume. And when they find them, they're going to kill, steal, and destroy them.

But we have never heard this story in context. For if we had, we would have known that the enemy that the Bible speaks of, which comes to kill, steal, and destroy, was actually our shepherds. Jesus is leveling us with the understanding that the middlemen we have placed as spiritual guides have actually been stumbling blocks to us getting to truly experience God.

Jesus Himself is telling us that those shepherds are up to no good. Their motives and intentions are all wrong. And He even tells us what their motives and intentions are: *money*!! And that is why, as a culture, it has been difficult for us to break free from this spiritual abuse and bondage, because those diabolical leaders have used fear to make you buy into their necessity.

Insidious leaders do not just steal for money. Jesus said they kill, steal, and destroy. Trust me, fraudulent leaders do exactly that. They kill character, individuality, purpose, creativity, hope, and true identity.

This may very well be why, as a people, African Americans have not grown to the level we should have. This is why our people are withering away in religious organizations, never becoming business magnets, moguls, or CEOs of major corporations. We have listened to outside sources for our identity, and they caused us to adopt a reality that is not truly ours.

Christ reveals His desire and plans for us in John 10. He said, "A thief is only there to steal and kill and destroy. I came so they can have real and eternal life, more and better life than they ever dreamed of." He identified for us what the enemy came to do and what His plan was as an alternative.

Christ wants you to have a real life. Not an imitation of Righteousness in which your Sunday morning wardrobe gives you away. His desire is for you to have a life that is real, authentic, and genuine. The shepherds that you have set up in your lives are direct adversaries to those plans.

But still you won't listen to Christ Consciousness because you've been convinced that those leaders have been ordained and sanctioned by God. African American communities will never grow and manifest the greatness that we lost until we return our awareness to our true identity. Believe me, we were not always slaves, nor did we always adopt a slave psychology.

I am aware that there was a time in history when this type of leadership served our people tremendously. We have received our cues from some great and dynamic religious leaders, who heralded the brilliance of our design. However, over the course of history, our religious leaders turned to greed and left behind the concept of community. They turned the Bible into a weapon and used it villainously toward so many groups of people, whom they chose not to understand. That type of teaching hypnotized our people into believing that religious devotion is God's highest ambition for us.

That kind of constant religious idol worship has kept us preoccupied and left us out of the evolutionary social and economic growth process.

The longer we hold this delusional concept of relationship with God, the longer poverty will be our constant companion. Dumbed down religious leaders target messages at specific groups, alienating the very people who are full of wisdom, whom we need to hear from within this generation.

We truly have "One Father," and religious entities are no longer being allowed to hold that Father hostage. We can no longer allow religious leaders to create hostile environments by excluding from the Gospel message anyone they deem unworthy. God is the Father of all of us, whether or not the religious leaders recognize that.

> *At that moment, the temple curtain was ripped in two, top to bottom.* (Matthew 27:51)

We get teary eyed over this knowledge that the veil was ripped in the temple, signaling to us that we no longer needed a high priest. That rip in the veil granted us direct access to the throne of God. Yet, we keep attempting to sew up that curtain and use it as a veil for security.

Matthew 27:51 basically champions the message that we no longer need a middleman between us and God. Yet, we constantly believe the blatant contradiction that the middleman connects us to God. However, this generation knows better.

Our relationship with God no longer has to be enforced by some spiritual bodyguard—an enforcer who thinks that he or she knows what is best for me without even knowing my personal experience and journey. So long as we continue with this flawed construct of spiritual relationship, we will continue to force ourselves to relive and rebuild primitive foundations of separateness that produce no fruit. Holding on to such a contradiction to the original plan of Christ for our lives is an act that defies our very nature.

This middleman relationship has replaced the work that you need to do on yourself. You pay your tithes, and that's enough. You obey your pastor, and God will elevate you. That is how dumbed down we have made our relationship with God. We have made knowing God as easy as getting your pastor's approval and validation.

I understand that I am offering concepts that totally challenge you to examine yourself. My idea is for you to grow and mature so that you can create real change in your personal life. Once you do that, you can change the way you project yourself in your community, ultimately changing it for the better.

Moving beyond the need for low-level leadership will not only cause you to grow and change, but you just may inspire the men and women you call spiritual fathers and mothers to grow by finding out what it is they themselves should be doing at this time.

You may actually help them to release themselves from the burdens they have taken on themselves. By assuming the role of middlemen between God and humanity, they have assumed a role that God never assigned to them. For many of these figureheads, trying to keep dead, dry, institutional churches alive is costing them their very own lives. Let's not forget:

> *Good understanding giveth favor: but the way of the transgressors is hard.* (Proverbs 13:15)

It is hard to live a lie, and it's even harder to live that lie in the name of God. Many fraudulent spiritual leaders were elected by the people, but not selected by God. They can very easily be consumed by the pressures of keeping up with the fraudulent images they have created for themselves.

So many of these fraudulent leaders walk with arrogant pride, refusing to admit that they have wasted countless years, perhaps decades, in so-called ministry. They may have been successful for a time, until people awakened to their hypocrisy and theft. They hold on to their sinking ships all the way to the bottom.

But I want to give some of you leaders a way out from your self-inflicted misery. That misery is certainly self-inflicted because pastor, bishop, and apostle were not merely titles that God created to appoint people to be spiritual guides. That's a misinterpretation of Biblical text.

The religious system was set up, designed, and reinforced with rules that don't allow for intellect, wisdom, or sound counsel. The moment we encounter real organic wisdom, we are taught to demonize it as the wisdom of this world, totally forgetting, in our ignorance, that God is Omniscient. That is, She knows everything, possesses all knowledge and all science. Jesus offered religious leaders a simple solution to their delicate dilemma:

> *Don't let people maneuver you into taking charge of them. There is only one Life-Leader for you and them—Christ. Do you want to stand out? Then step down, be a servant.* (Matthew 23:10-11)

First of all, you must admit that you have placed yourselves in a position in people's lives that you were never intended to be. You have allowed yourselves to police and profit from God's people. You have created laws, rules, and rituals that have nothing to do with God's plan for humanity. You have led God's people ignorantly, with no true knowledge or understanding of the Bible that you claim to defend.

If you can ever give up your arrogant pride and deception, the Bible says, "Step Down!" This is the part of "We Have One Father" that they don't want to hear. They think it is better for them to be propped up in a worthless position than to give up their delusions. Most of them will *never* step down, because those fraudulent titles and positions have given them their identity.

What would they do, and who would they be, if they didn't have the pulpits that give them their identity? Some of you might say, "What about the ones who have been so philanthropic and given to their communities?" I'm certain there are many of those loving people. In fact, I've met quite a few. However, you can have a kind and generous heart and still be misguided in your purpose.

We have become complacent about groups and governments that give us assistance of various kinds, financial and otherwise, but never give us the truth that makes us free. We will always have to create welfare systems until the people see themselves as they should. If spiritual leaders actually taught a message that gave value to their listeners, people would not need mere philanthropic assistance. Instead, they would elevate their economic status based on knowing their intrinsic worth and value.

Ignorant followers of religious frauds are valuable in religious systems that God did not create as unlearned accomplices in their own demise. For them, darkness will fight light at all cost. You will know the truth from the lies easily. All you have to do is remember that one message enslaves, the other sets you free. The real message of Christ is to liberate you and set you free. The message of the church and religion is to enslave and to bind you.

CHAPTER 12

The Mystery of the Gospel!

The Law saith, Where is thy Righteousness, goodness, and satisfaction? The Gospel saith, Christ is thy Righteousness, goodness, and satisfaction.

—Patrick Hamilton

BEFORE I EVEN give a Biblical reference to oblige the religious, to prove what I'm saying is truth, may I just say, ironically, that I had to leave organized religion to discover exactly what Jesus' purpose and mission truly were. I certainly had to leave to discover just how too-good-to-be-true the message of Christ truly is.

I never knew how much a conversation I had with myself, in front of a church in Brooklyn, would impact my life and lead me on such a discovery and journey. I wanted to get to the bottom of why God was villainously angry with people who didn't have my fundamental religious beliefs, or even didn't have *any* religious beliefs at all. My question inspired God to create experiences in my life that led me to the truth.

Most of those experiences, I might add, were painful ones. However, my current awareness has taught me that much of my suffering was caused by negative concepts that were not even my own. Yet, I lived them out in my reality, and they caused me to self-sabotage most of my life. Furthermore, my immaturity caused me to deal treacherously with others in relationships.

But at some point, most mature adults must assume responsibility for their own lives and begin to rectify the negative concepts and ideologies they have lived by. No matter what area of life you have allowed such negative ideologies to destroy, this chapter will help you to rectify one of the most misleading of Christianity's religious dogmas. However, some readers may consider this chapter controversial and perhaps even misleading.

Creating false doctrines and living them out as truth hinders God's genuine intentions for humanity. Those false doctrines that we have created have caused major conflicts throughout human history. Yet, we continue to practice them as truth.

Religious people have claimed to lead others to find the message of God's love, yet they have unintentionally kept those others from experiencing it. For centuries now, those religious people have denied themselves the freedom to truly and fully experience God's love, because they don't even know the profundity of its significance.

The average churchgoer has only experienced religion's watered down version. Let's never forget, religion can only tell you where God *was!* Spirituality reveals where She *is!* That is why religion has become a mundane ritual carried out in the name of God, offering nothing but empty rituals and obligations.

The search for God through rituals leads everywhere except within yourself. However, you ask, When do we ever reach the destination? We don't! And that is because religion is the only institution of learning from which we were never intended to graduate.

Within the African American religious community, members have assumed all the titles they could possibly take within the church, without ever growing beyond the institution to truly create something great in the world. Worst of all, they have never truly experienced themselves as they really are, because they have created a doctrine that prefers being right to being real.

That is why Jesus called religious people hypocrites, "having a form of Godliness and denying the power thereof" (II Timothy 3:5). That form of Godliness comforts those people even in their disobedience of God's truth. They dismiss the truth away, and justify doing that by saying their lies are in Her name. Therefore, they will continue to blindly and ignorantly say to themselves, "I am standing on the word of God!"

What they truly mean is that they are going to stand on their twisted interpretation of God's word, so that they can continue to live the lie. Even if they rip this book to shreds, the message of God's love will still be true. But God is awakening the remnant—that is, the very few who refuse to bow to the fake and fraudulent systems of this world—to truly restore Christ Consciousness.

The doctrine for which Spirit has designed this chapter is The Gospel. Who was it really for? By religious standards, especially Christian standards, we must assume that the Gospel was just for a few who adopt Christian concepts, philosophies, ideologies, and dogmas.

Yet, so-called believers will disagree with me, saying that the Gospel message is for everyone. However, only a few will accept *their* version of it, and be accepted into their faith. In their verbiage they say everyone, yet in their practice they mean only a few.

Those who practice a narrow version of Christianity are forbidden to question the real message of the Gospel of Christ. The delusional concepts they have about Jesus are defended away by them saying, "It can't be understood with secular knowledge or conventional wisdom. The Gospel of Christ must be understood spiritually." However, according to narrow-minded Christians, you must become one of them in order to understand that Gospel. I have been a Christian my whole life, so I can assure you, their version of Christianity makes no sense.

According to religious people, you must have a preacher scream at you for forty-five minutes in order to understand the Gospel. But if the church's gospel message is really true, why do they need all of the learned charismatic behaviors and theatrics to deliver that message? Can the truth not stand on its own? Is a search for Jesus as simple as going to the neighborhood church, and repeating some words after the preacher?

I don't mean to sound condescending. I simply want the reader to think a little. It is grievous to go to the house of bread, and find the cupboard bare. Jesus cursed a fig tree because it bore no fruit. Well, beloved, some of you have become that barren tree.

Today, religion is that tree, propped up but producing no fruit. It has only proven to be the "father of lies" and massive Biblical deceptions. But way too many Christians are afraid to even speak about religion's abusive tirade against God's true people. Narrow-minded Christians have literally turned the message of Christ on its head, so that it has no effect. They have even become comfortable with using Jesus to push and promote their political agendas, while never committing to the basic tenets of their faith: love, fairness, tolerance, and justice.

And they have done all of this while comfortably saying, "Lord! Lord!" They use God as a bully to punish all the people who don't think, believe, or behave like them. The Gospel of organized religion forces people to give up their truest identities to conform to identities expected of them by others. But the Gospel is *not* some message that can be used to force people to live according to other people's interpretations.

The Gospel of organized religion is sinful because it robs people of an organic and natural relationship with the divine. A genuine relationship with God must be private.

Organized religion has held the Gospel of Christ hostage and then incorrectly distributed it around the Earth. That is why I stood at the door of the church in Brooklyn, wondering why some people were alienated from my fundamentalist Gospel message. Why, I wondered, were they destined for Hell and utter destruction, simply because they didn't subscribe to my understanding of God?

The answer to that question, and so many more, is that it wasn't true and never was! Rather, it was my limited and primitive religious understanding that caused me to mistakenly believe falsehood as truth. My indoctrination in false doctrines caused me to see the message of Christ through a distorted lens, which made it virtually impossible for most people to ever know Him—at least according to what I assumed "knowing Him" meant.

Because it is a blatant lie and contradiction to the life that God intended for you, religion will always distort the truth to fit its control over your life. Religion will teach you to see everyone whose religious beliefs are different from yours as outsiders who are alienated from the Gospel message.

Those "outsiders" disqualify themselves from receiving God's love by choosing to live deviant and defiant lives. Narrow-minded religious people believe they are in the Kingdom of God, while the outsiders are in the pit. That ideology prevents narrow-minded religious people from seeing the beauty in the world, believing that God just wanted things in black and white.

Good news is what the prophet Isaiah prophesied, and Jesus fulfilled. He became the living example of God's love.

> *God's Spirit is on me; he's chosen me to preach the Message of good news to the poor, sent me to announce pardon to prisoners and recovery of sight to the blind, to set the burdened and battered free, to announce, "This is God's year to act!"* (Luke 4:18)

This is good news! It is a prophecy of what Jesus would actually do. This entire prophecy of the Gospel of Luke tells us that Jesus' intention is to set people free! Not only does He want to set people free, but He also wants to restore sight to the blind! The Gospel message is to get us to see clearly. It does not offer a distorted view that makes excuses for slavery.

The Gospel of Christ was not intended just to set people free from the consciousness of sin; it was intended to set us *totally* free—especially from religious dogmas and doctrines. Now that we have freed ourselves to see the Gospel of Christ correctly, let's look at what the Book of Ephesians says about the mystery of Christ's message:

> *The mystery is that people who have never heard of God and those who have heard of him all their lives (what I've been calling outsiders and insiders) stand on the same ground before God. They get the same offer, same help, same promises in Christ Jesus. The Message is accessible and welcoming to everyone, across the board.* (Ephesians 3:6)

That's plain and simple English! No tricks! No gimmicks! Narrow-minded religious people have missed what the mystery of the Gospel actually is. In their indoctrinations, they teach people to be Anti-Christs. In so doing, they have adopted a gospel of exclusion instead of one of inclusion. They have done that in their vain need to control who they say can accept Christ.

This separation into insiders and outsiders has allowed them to see themselves as a righteous elite and everyone else as vagrants. Thankfully, no matter what their delusional concepts have been, or will continue to be, we know now that Christ Consciousness is all about inclusion. Narrow-minded religious people believe that it's too good to be true that God made room for everyone.

The Gospel is a mystery, not because we have to speak in tongues to comprehend it, but because it is difficult for some people to fathom that God so loved the World that he would send His Son to save it. That Son honored the mission of love by making room for everyone.

For those of you who continue to defend your narrow-minded delusion by saying that this is heresy, and you are keeping the highest standards, I must ask, Whose standards are you keeping? Certainly not the standards of Christ. God's Son made room for the insiders and the outsiders to be on equal ground to get the same promises from the Father. No one is greater than anyone else or more deserving of God's promises. Everyone gets an equal chance to experience love in a real and viable way, but not because of anything that we have done.

Fall Back! This Has Nothing to Do with You!

Saving is all his [i.e., God's] idea, and all his work. All we do is trust him enough to let him do it. It's God's gift from start to finish! We don't play the major role. If we did, we'd probably go around bragging that we'd done

> *the whole thing! No, we neither make nor save ourselves. God does both the making and saving. He creates each of us by Christ Jesus to join him in the work he does, the good work he has gotten ready for us to do, work we had better be doing.* (Ephesians 2:8-10)

Narrow-minded religious people have literally changed "For God so loved the world" to "For God so loved *some* of the world." And they have also changed "He sent not his Son into the world to condemn the world" to "He sent his Son to condemn most of the world except for a few." This distortion was created to enslave and manipulate people's true identity, and has hindered so many people from experiencing the fullness of their own creation.

This message of separation is one that religion villainously upholds, and governments vigorously finance. Being able to label some individuals as right and others as wrong has allowed religious leaders to demonize entire communities, simply because they don't understand them, or because they choose to profit off the ignorant. As their defense, they boldly use the name of God and the purpose of Christ.

It was not outsiders who distorted a true organic relationship with God. It was the religious communities! The so-called body of Christ stood in the way of everything that is full and free. They denied so many from experiencing a full life in Christ.

Narrow-minded religious people took control of the Gospel message and held it hostage. They appointed themselves "Defenders of the faith," picking and choosing who they felt was deserving of their message.

None of us has anything to do with the work of salvation. This was "God's gift to us, from start to finish." Yet, somehow we have been taught to believe that salvation is about us, or about the rigorous work we have done in the name of Christianity. Or we believe that the Gospel has been released to our care, custody, and control. How can that be when the Gospel was a gift that had nothing to do with any of us?

How have we forgotten that "it's not by works, lest any of us could boast"? That is exactly what we have become: a society that believes an individual should be celebrated for his or her religious devotion—that is, for how well he or she has kept others from experiencing the Gospel. We must find better examples of spiritual leadership for ourselves. Religious devotion has been a roadblock to real experience.

What actually needs to happen is that narrow-minded religious people need to fall back, because the Gospel has nothing to do with them. They have taken the freedom and joy out of the gift—not to mention the miserable life they have created for themselves, living contrary to the purpose and design of God for their lives. Jesus never needed to be defended. Nor did He ever search for devotion from anyone.

That would have nullified the whole purpose for His coming. There is no way to enjoy a relationship that always needs defending. Jesus never came to prove that He was the best choice for savior. Nor did He come with the idea that everyone would believe in Him. He came to demonstrate a love that would radically change the world—if it were ever experienced individually.

From start to finish, Jesus' message is not about us. His message requires no work of us! No rigorous and strenuous blind devotion. No contracts to sign and no churches to join. All we have to do is trust that He handled *all* of the details.

Ephesians 2:8-10 gives us a clear way to escape all these responsibilities. It shows that the responsibility for salvation was never on us. It also reminds us that no one has the right to lord his or her religious devotions over another. I did not write this book to give the so-called "degenerates" of the world the right to be degenerate, or to debate who was or was not deserving of Jesus' Gospel.

I did, however, want to make it clear that those who have stood in the way of the Gospel were liars! Jesus' Gospel made room for insiders and outsiders without their permission or say-so. By God's generous gift of His son, He proved that love covers us, even before we knew that we needed covering. And it covers us even if we go for our entire lives, never knowing that we needed it. That is Unconditional Love!

Just how diabolical our understanding of God has been has stunned me ever since I left organized religion. Our dogmas are truly steeped in ignorance. Worse yet, they have a terribly negative impact on families and entire communities, and they have negatively influenced government with watered down unfounded religious rhetoric.

Our diabolical understanding of God has incapacitated so many people from seeing themselves as they should. It's a mental illness that needs to be cured. And it is easily cured by applying this next verse to our lives:

> So here's what I want you to do, God
> helping you: Take your everyday, ordinary

> *life—your sleeping, eating, going-to-work, and walking-around life—and place it before God as an offering. Embracing what God does for you is the best thing you can do for him. Don't become so well-adjusted to your culture that you fit into it without even thinking. Instead, fix your attention on God. You'll be changed from the inside out. Readily recognize what he wants from you, and quickly respond to it. Unlike the culture around you, always dragging you down to its level of immaturity, God brings the best out of you, develops well-formed maturity in you.* (Romans 12:1-2)

Until now, I have never read this verse in the Message translation. But I simply wanted to show you that the diabolical understanding of God could be fixed by the "renewing of your mind"—that is, by changing the way you see yourself in relationship to God. Paul said to just take your everyday life and recognize what God has done for you.

> *Everybody dies in Adam; everybody comes alive in Christ.* (1 Cor. 15:22)

We have delusionally believed that, by eating of the tree, Adam introduced man to sin and damnation, and that everyone born after him is doomed with a sin problem—even after God sent His son into the world.

It is delusional to believe that Adam could damn all men, but the "Perfect Lamb" is powerless to redeem them all! As Paul said in Romans 12:1-2: "Don't be so caught up with your culture that you fit in without even thinking. Instead, fix your attention on God. You'll be changed from the inside out."

Narrow-minded religious people declare "God" from their religious headquarters. Yet, they never allow Him to change them from the inside out. That requires work and responsibility. It forces them to deal with the concepts they have created for themselves and the prisons they have created for others by neglecting to see them after the spirit, while judging and passing judgments solely after the flesh.

Hopefully, by now, you are beginning to see just how ineffective you have made the message of Christ by building religious houses on delusions, and not on Christ Consciousness. "Except the Lord build the house," says Psalms 127:1, "they labor in vain that build it: except the Lord keep the city, the watchman wakes in vain."

CHAPTER 13

Law Breakers!

The law will never make men free, it is men that have to make the law free.

—Henry David Thoreau

MOST PEOPLE BELIEVE in the notion of "free will." They have preached it. They have taught it. They have credited God with creating "free will" as a character design in all humans, to help them navigate this human experience. However, let's examine the definition of *free will*.

> *Free will* (noun): voluntary choice or decision ("I do this of my own free will"); freedom of humans to make choices that

are not determined by prior causes or by divine intervention.

As with many other words and phrases, the religious have distorted the very meaning of the words *free will*. To begin with, they have placed restrictions on it, most of those restrictions steeped in condemnation.

For example, they say, in effect: "You do in fact have free will. However, if you don't use that free will to find *our* version of truth, you are destined for destruction, and Hell certainly awaits you." That is such a heinous and biased depiction of God's love toward us.

Many religious individuals have said that young people today simply want to live any way they choose without anyone telling them differently. And, in essence, that is true—but not in the perverted way that the accusers have in mind, due to their primitive understanding of Biblical text.

> *What is the point, then, of the law, the attached addendum? It was a thoughtful addition to the original covenant promises made to Abraham. The purpose of the law was to keep a sinful people in the way of salvation until Christ (the descendant) came,*

> *inheriting the promises and distributing them to us. Obviously this law was not a firsthand encounter with God. It was arranged by angelic messengers through a middleman, Moses. But if there is a middleman as there was at Sinai, then the people are not dealing directly with God, are they? But the original promise is the direct blessing of God, received by faith.* (Galatians 3:18-20)

Young people are coming to understand and redefine "free will," not out of a sheer desire to pervert what it means to be in relationship or communion with God. There is a minority of them who are actually seeking to put relationship with God back into its proper perspective. And they are doing that by putting the law into perspective.

Young people today understand the weakness in relationship with God through the law. Yet, that is not a new understanding, because Paul put a heavy indictment on attempting to be in relationship with God by way of the law, and he became more opposed to it as time went on. We can see this clearly in Romans 7:

> *Don't you remember how it was? I do,*
> *perfectly well. The law code started out as*
> *an excellent piece of work. What happened,*
> *though, was that sin found a way to pervert the*
> *command into a temptation, making a piece*
> *of "forbidden fruit" out of it. The law code,*
> *instead of being used to guide me, was used*
> *to seduce me. Without all the paraphernalia*
> *of the law code, sin looked pretty dull and*
> *lifeless, and I went along without paying*
> *much attention to it. But once sin got its*
> *hands on the law code and decked itself out*
> *in all that finery, I was fooled, and fell for it.*
> (Romans 7:8-11)

Paul wrestled with the law, realizing that trying to keep it actually created the appetite to sin. It awakened him to the other side of his creation. Remember, the information of both good and evil existed simultaneously within the same tree (The Tree of the Knowledge of Good and Evil). In Romans 7, Paul begins to realize that as long as he paid the law no attention, sin became more powerful.

The power of sin emerged when people surrendered right relationship with Christ Consciousness:

> *The very command that was supposed to guide me into life was cleverly used to trip me up, throwing me headlong. So sin was plenty alive, and I was stone dead.* (Romans 7:10-11)

This is a very clear and vivid depiction of today's religious institutions, in which people commit themselves to being slaves to the law and to enslaving others to it. In their own communities, sin is very much alive, while they are very much dead. They believe that their religious devotions and conformity to a secondhand knowledge of Christ Consciousness is a crown that should be celebrated as righteousness.

The very thing (the Law) that they have used to govern and direct their lives, has tripped them up. That is why Jesus called the religious community hypocrites, because that is the only thing that this secondhand encounter with the divine could possibly produce. Paul later cleared this up in Galatians, by which time he had clearly evolved in his understanding.

> *Obviously [Mosaic] law was not a firsthand encounter with God. It was arranged by angelic messengers through a middleman, Moses.* (Galatians 3:19)

Let's be clear. We must understand how unjust and irrelevant Biblical law is today. But for many narrow-minded religious people, the measure of their love has been determined by the laws they have created for themselves. They have total disdain for a myriad of communities based on their interpretations of the law, and they bind others to adopt their primitive understanding of love based on the law. They even sometimes feel justified when harm comes to any of those communities, believing that God has, in some way, wreaked havoc on His enemies and theirs.

That is such a distorted and perverted understanding of "For God so loved the World!" Those narrow-minded religious people have destroyed families by causing them to believe that God only intended for them to have contact with individuals who think and believe like them. That is the work of diabolical religious leaders who stand as middlemen, interrupting a pure pursuit of Christ Consciousness.

Let's look again at that verse in Galatians:

> *What is the point, then, of the law, the attached addendum? It was a thoughtful addition to the original covenant promises made to Abraham. The purpose of the law*

> *was to keep a sinful people in the way of salvation until Christ (the descendant) came, inheriting the promises and distributing them to us. Obviously this law was not a firsthand encounter with God. It was arranged by angelic messengers through a middleman, Moses. But if there is a middleman as there was at Sinai, then the people are not dealing directly with God, are they? But the original promise is the direct blessing of God, received by faith.* (Galatians 3:18-20)

Paul said that Mosaic law was arranged by a middleman, Moses. But if there is a middleman, the people are not dealing directly with God, are they? That is why there is a rapid decline in religious attendance. That is why so many congregations around the country lie barren and in waste. Not because people are leaving God, but Christ Consciousness has caught up with the times and is forcing this change.

It's a virtual impossibility to have a genuine relationship with God through middlemen. Yet, this is the culture in which so many people have deified religious leaders as sacred, not knowing that they are a blatant interruption to a natural and organic relationship with God.

> *You crazy Galatians! Did someone put a hex on you? Have you taken leave of your senses? Something crazy has happened, for it's obvious that you no longer have the crucified Jesus in clear focus in your lives. His sacrifice on the cross was certainly set before you clearly enough. Let me put this question to you: How did your new life begin?*
>
> *Was it by working your heads off to please God? Or was it by responding to God's Message to you? Are you going to continue this craziness? For only crazy people would think they could complete by their own efforts what was begun by God. If you weren't smart enough or strong enough to begin it, how do you suppose you could perfect it?*
> (Galatians 3:1-3)

Oh, you crazy institutional church and organized religion! You have clearly lost sight of Christ Consciousness. If salvation were as simple as us believing that Christ completed the mission, and believing that the work of Christ truly "is finished," how did things get so complicated?

This brings me back to my own experience with organized religion, growing up as a young man indoctrinated in the African American Church. Not only did religion consume over half of my life, but it was a tedious and strenuous obligation, a consistent struggle to live up to everyone else's standards for my life. Through an abundance of fear, I was forced to believe that the middlemen held my divine destiny. And that is still the fraudulent teaching of many churches: that God has required us to keep all of the rituals, rules, and laws, without knowing that it is middlemen who act as thought police, making sure I follow all of their commands.

I believed that by taking that spiritual abuse, I would get closer to God. But all that did for me was lead me in an endless search for validation and approval from people who never really mattered to me. Wrongly seeing those middlemen as spiritual fathers denied me access to the very thing that was full and free: a genuine relationship with God.

That fraudulent moral code has produced people who not only have *not* experienced real Christ Consciousness, but have actually denied themselves the right to know who they are. I still sit and watch friends and even family members who live this lie. They keep up with appearances for the approval of others, believing that is what is necessary to grow in God. Sadly, they never get to be honest and to tell the truth about their identities.

Some people have been living in this delusional state for so long that they have no idea where they are anymore. There are so many miserable marriages, relationships, and covenants built from lies and pretenses in the name of God.

Narrow-minded religious people have doctored sermons to foster fear that will prevent anyone from ever speaking out against such grievous acts. Again, middlemen are considered sacred and divine—God's men and women here on Earth to lead and guide us. That is why we continue to hear sermons that reinforce the position of the leaders rather than the people.

Followers are conditioned to defend this position, even when the position has no real purpose. Real spiritual leaders never need to usurp their authority over others. They only want to help you to discover your true identity in Christ Consciousness. They never lord it over you as your superiors, but realize that we are all classmates and have only one Father!

This is the model that real Christ Consciousness brings to humanity. If you are truly created in the image and likeness of God, what additions do you need? Isn't an awareness of being created in His image and likeness sufficient? If we are truly created in His image and likeness, then no one can ever lord his or her identity, beliefs, and ideas over another. We are *all* divine.

The time is *now* for young people to become law breakers! I'm not talking about state and federal laws (although the time may arise for that, too). I'm talking from a deeper spiritual level. We must break this diabolical secondhand account with God, because it has literally set back and stagnated generations. When we do not allow people to truly walk in and through their divinity, we stagnate creativity.

If anything is needed now, it is a burst of fresh air—new ideas, modalities, and behaviors that truly allow us to live and walk in love!

> *Are you going to continue this craziness? For only crazy people would think they could complete by their own efforts what was begun by God. If you weren't smart enough or strong enough to begin it, how do you suppose you could perfect it?* (Galatians 3:3)

Now, seriously! Do you think that you could complete a work that neither you nor I was smart or strong enough to begin? By committing to tedious patterns of religious devotion, you have stagnated, blocking yourself from becoming who you are truly supposed to be. That is why most of us have no real goals or aspirations outside of our religious institution.

Our religious leaders have allowed us to settle for mediocrity and intellectual poverty, persuading us to believe that we only deserve a good job, a nice house, a comfortable car, and maybe a loving spouse. In that way, we never fully grasp who we truly are from the inside out. Trust me, you are brilliant by design. Yet, you will never truly know that until you quit this narrow-minded legal craziness!

A belief is simply an idea that is continually practiced and rehearsed. That does not make the belief correct. Therefore, when that belief does not call you to your "higher self," it is time to discard it, even if it is one of your most fundamental dogmas.

> *That is the way it is with us: When we were minors, we were just like slaves ordered around by simple instructions (the tutors and*

> *administrators of this world), with no say in*
> *the conduct of our own lives.* (Galatians 4:3)

Take Your Life Back!

Always keep one thing in mind: Slavery enslaves, but Christ Consciousness will always make you free.

Our contemporary culture has made everything that is full and free a lie, and has perverted our roles in one another's lives. In fact, we have adopted an anti-Christ Consciousness in our religious doctrines and practices. A middleman relationship with God always requires one to be above others—as in the religious leader being above the followers. That perversion of brotherly love has forced the subservient ones to forfeit their identity in order to maintain the identity created for them by the dominant one.

That is not the role that Christ Consciousness intends for you. There was definitely a period in my life when I needed to be under tutors and instructors. But at some point, when I became an adult, I had to take control over my own life. That's when I discovered that my primitive beliefs were not serving me. I was spiraling out of control in the abyss of contradictory opinions about myself. And none of those opinions were even my own!

I had to use the "free will" that God created in our design to reprogram myself away from every religious falsehood. It is foolish to believe that without moral codes and ritual devotion, we don't know how to conduct ourselves morally. With or without a religious foundation, love in its purest form is more than sufficient to teach us how to behave.

The middleman religious relationship fosters unworthiness and separation, always requiring an outside influence to give us value and worth. In truth, the moment I began to love myself enough to speak out against spiritual abuse, I was banished from the narrow-minded religious kingdom—because the very nature of that rigid relationship is to stagnate and subvert self-worth and self-love. However, the longer we remain ignorant and voiceless, the longer the middlemen's reign of terror over us lasts.

We all have a moral obligation to grow and evolve in our understanding, so that from our very being we can create experiences that uplift us within this human existence. We can do that by comprehending that our experiences are the truth, and the religious leaders are the falsehoods.

When we truly begin to break free from the laws, dogmas, and rituals that have held us captive, scales will fall from our eyes, and we will see just how valuable we truly are. For many of you, this message will be liberating enough to restore sight to you in an instant. You will recall moments in your life when you allowed someone else's religious opinions to shape your identity and control how you see and experience the world.

But right now, you can see just how diabolical that secondhand encounter with God has been. As those scales begin to fall from your eyes, you may become angry when you think about how many years of your life you have given to those negative behaviors. But that's alright. You will get over it!

> *That's why I don't think there's any comparison between the present hard times and the coming good times. The created world itself can hardly wait for what's coming next. Everything in creation is being more or less held back. God reins it in until both creation and all the creatures are ready and can be released at the same moment into the glorious times ahead. Meanwhile, the joyful anticipation deepens.* (Romans 18:19-21)

Real freedom is never easy. It comes with great sacrifice. But freedom is always worth it! When I first came to this understanding, I was truly freed by it. And from my misery, God created a ministry. I don't say that lightly, or as a cliché, because my misery was the African American Church.

If we don't take our lives back, African American communities will continue to suffer. We will never see each other in love as we should, and that divisiveness will always stir up chaos and strife. We must take back our lives and begin to work out our souls' salvation. We should not do that by basing our beliefs on a book, a theology, religious leaders, parents, teachers, friends, or social media, but on what works for our real lives, not the illusions we have created to impress the outside world.

Our lives will never turn in the direction they should, no matter how much we shout, pray, or beg, unless and until we discard our illusions. But seeing ourselves as we should is a journey we have to take alone. Yet, what we discover about ourselves will so liberate us that we will never again settle for anyone or anything that does not reflect the beauty of our design.

You will never settle in your life for relationships that are not open, honest, and true. You will no longer allow manipulation and spiritual abuse to control or dictate your life's experiences. You will never again seek to manipulate or control those people you are blessed to encounter on this journey. Taking back your life and walking in true Christ Consciousness will always cause you to find value in others, never reinforcing anything that devalues them.

I would like to conclude this chapter with this extremely powerful verse:

> *I am emphatic about this. The moment any one of you submits to circumcision or any other rule-keeping system, at that same moment Christ's hard-won gift of freedom is squandered. I repeat my warning: The person who accepts the ways of circumcision trades all the advantages of the free life in Christ for the obligations of the slave life of the law.* (Galatians 5:2-3)

In plain English, scripture warns us against submitting to the slave life, which literally squanders away true and natural Christ Consciousness. We have made it hard for ourselves to have a relationship and covenant with God and each other that is full and free!

We have dedicated years to a religious system that Christ Consciousness never designed—a religious system that was birthed after Adam's fall in consciousness. We have given millions, if not billions, of dollars to that religious system, instead of being awakened by Christ Consciousness to use those dollars to develop our own communities.

This is not just some message to tickle your fancy, to jump on the bandwagon of some new doctrine. Not at all, brothers and sisters! This is a prophetic warning that we must break free from this system of oppression, so that we work diligently on reversing this self-hatred, self-loathing, self-condemning, self-devaluing relationship that we have had for centuries with the divine.

Because we have demonized intellect and wisdom within religious settings, we have caused ourselves to be ensnared by our own ignorance, thus preventing our own advancement. And all the while, we have done it in the name of God, calling it service unto God. This delusional understanding has prevented us from thinking about our community, and kept us focused on ourselves instead, which has caused us to overlook the need to celebrate and support our own.

Narrow-minded religious people have been spending centuries judging the world, condemning it for the very things they have done themselves and still do in their own churches. They judge entire communities because those communities are bold enough to walk in freedom. Narrow-minded religious people waste a monumental amount of time getting exposed and then covering it up. They elevate the accused while they lavish in the offense of their brothers and sisters. One of them commits a sin, and they make him a bishop.

We all have a moral obligation to stand for justice for everybody, so that no one is left feeling judged and condemned. We have a moral obligation not only to say the word *love*, but to express it. Let's not forget, love was Jesus' purpose and mission on Earth. Therefore, love must also be *our* purpose and mission.

CHAPTER 14

Freedom, the New Heresy!

The most important kind of freedom is to be what you really are. You trade in your reality for a role. You trade in your sense for an act. You give up your ability to feel, and in exchange, put on a mask. There can't be any large-scale revolution until there's a personal revolution, on an individual level. It's got to happen inside first.

—Jim Morrison

HERE I AM in the penultimate chapter before I conclude this book, releasing it into the universe to say or do what needs to be said or done. Perhaps in this chapter, the Holy Spirit will allow me to be a little more candid about my own personal experiences, which have led me to my present understanding of God.

I must admit that rehashing experiences that have gotten me to this space has proven at times to be very difficult. That is not because I don't remember the experiences or because many of them were horrific. I have just grown so much in my understanding and in my divinity that I am no longer emotionally attached to those experiences. I only retain from them the lessons I have learned. I do know that I would not trade one step of the journey for anything, no matter how difficult the test proved to be.

At the onset of this book, I said that this journey has led me right back to myself. Like Adam, the first man, I realized that I was hiding from God. I was hiding from my very own divinity! Believing that I was unworthy made me act in ways that proved I *was*. As I noted earlier, my pedigree is steeped in the African American Pentecostal Church, which is a highly judgmental, condemning, angry, and spiritually abusive community.

I grew up in a home that knew everything about church and religion—a preacher's kid, who ended up being a preacher himself. But somehow my family knew absolutely *nothing* about having a natural and organic relationship with one another. That meant that we behaved one way in church and another at home. And I'm not just seeing that dysfunction in my own family. I'm witnessing it all around me in that so-called family of believers. My beliefs, dogmas, and doctrines said one thing, and everyone else in the congregation said another.

From my early childhood, I was passionate about God and the human race. That wasn't a passion that was merely about church and doing things in church. I seriously wanted to know God and to be able to teach others about Him. On top of that passion, built inside of me, was something I call "being real." I couldn't pretend that an experience was not happening just because my dogma taught me to ignore it.

On Saturday, January 16, 1993, I never knew just how much my understanding of my relationship with God would begin to change. But I knew after that day that I would never be the same again. That was the day that my oldest brother, Donald, was shot and killed. Twenty-seven years later, not one single day goes by when he hasn't crossed my mind in some way. That moment in time changed me forever, and even then I knew something inside me had shifted.

However, to this day I do not know the motivation of the shooter, because I never wanted to hear about it. Every time someone in my family started to discuss that story, I would leave the room. All I know is that the shooter was a man who made the decision to take my brother's life, and pulling the trigger only took a moment.

On Sunday, January 24, 1993, the day after we laid my brother to rest, I remember the whole previous week as if it were yesterday, and I will probably never forget it. But on that Sunday, I was getting ready to take a shower to prepare for church that morning, when I sat down on the edge of the tub and broke down crying. I didn't even know how or where to resume my life. Donald was so much more to me than just a big brother. On so many levels, he was the man I most wanted to be like.

Most people who knew Donald thought he was a bad kid, but that was far from the truth. I haven't met many people who have the heart or compassion that Donald had, or the wisdom he possessed. He taught me to ask questions, and that lesson still works for me till this very day. In fact, it has led me to this book. In one single moment, I lost my best friend forever.

When I was sitting on the edge of that tub, Spirit said to me clearly, "I took your brother to reveal my purpose in and through you!"

That totally pissed me off! In that moment, I was furious with Spirit. At the time, I was a 16-year-old kid, and in my own understanding, there was no reason for someone who's called all-powerful to take my brother.

If He wanted to reveal something in and through me, that certainly didn't need my brother as a sacrifice—nor, at that point, was I really especially interested in knowing whatever it was that Spirit wanted to reveal to me. Yet, it was that moment in time that taught me not to be afraid to face the truth.

I realized that there was something sinister at work, and it was that diabolical behavior that led to my brother's death and also created a major internal conflict within me. As I said earlier, we were living one way at church, and another way at home. The negative physical and verbal abuse that I experienced in my home matched the spiritual abuse that I experienced at church.

How was it possible that the Bible could be used to validate the abuse I suffered at home and in church? The answer is that the archbishop instructed the church leaders to turn a blind eye to that physical and verbal abuse so that it didn't affect the image of the organization. I began to notice that we, "the body of believers," were a broken people, with all sorts of behavioral, psychological, abusive, sexually perverse, and manipulative control problems.

My brother losing his life woke me up to that delusion. Prior to that, I was just too young to explain it.

I honestly thought that my brother's death would break my passion for God and His people, but somehow it didn't. I continued my search for God, and wanted to know so much more about Him. But the more I searched and the more I understood, the more my religious leaders began to push me away.

The more my love and passion for humanity grew, the more I couldn't get with the con games in the back room of the church. Then the spiritual leaders started to character assassinate me in the front room. But even that never lessened my passion for God. I just didn't know that God was using all of these experiences to lead me outside of my religious confines, to truly experience Christ Consciousness.

Outside that church in Brownsville, Brooklyn, I saw the ruined families that we were creating in the "kingdom." I saw the young men and women we were exposing to homosexuality, and then demonizing and damning them to Hell, while abusing them sexually right inside the church.

I saw the young women that we were marrying to closeted homosexual men. Yet, we ignored it for the sake of keeping up the image of the church. I saw those so-called spiritual leaders committing infidelity without any consequences. I'm getting to why freedom is the new heresy! But let's dwell for a minute on the things that narrow-minded religious people have done to families, while continuing a new form of slavery.

I watched how the church leaders were sexually irresponsible, but *never* discussed sexually transmitted diseases within their "kingdom." They secretly lived all the things they demonized others for, while never recognizing the duality of their own divinity. Does that make them evil people worthy of death? Certainly not! But it does make them hypocritical.

I have no anger or malice toward anyone who has done me wrong or harm. Nor do I hold any malice or hatred for the sabotage I have done to myself. I was able to forgive my abusers by being able to forgive myself. It's taken me years to figure it out, but I finally realized that this was not just a case of people behaving badly. Something psychological was happening, and our dogmas and doctrines were at the center of it. As a young man, I couldn't explain it, but with all the abuse I was suffering, I knew that something was either wrong with God or seriously wrong with the way I perceived Him.

Something was seriously wrong with my being faithful to such a flawed system. To the best of my ability, I followed its rules, ethics, and moral codes, but the reality of what I was seeing in the lives of the congregants was totally different from what we were hollering and screaming about. How did we have such a "profound" message, yet such horrible personal lives?

How were the church members so anointed, and yet such proud, arrogant, manipulative, controlling, abusive, sexual deviants? Why were so many of the so-called "sacred heterosexual marriages" ending in divorce? Why were so many of our male leaders impregnating female members, yet never being challenged or questioned?

I knew at a very young age that something was flawed in the teachings of the church. The moment I began to ask certain questions, I was immediately branded a heretic. I most certainly was being heretical for challenging the traditions and the sacred middlemen who think for the system, because the leaders took pleasure in the power to control and manipulate the people.

I have always viewed leadership differently from the way the leaders do—not because I was trying to break the rules, but because I felt the effects of their diabolical abuse of power. Now that I'm older and more mature, I see just how damaging the effects of organized institutions are on our culture and community.

The number one curse over our lives that we need to break today is the curse of religious domination. *Freedom* has literally become one of the most popular words in the world today, because so many people are experiencing a fight for some form of freedom in their lives.

I no longer feel that in my life because I've learned to walk in Christ Consciousness. However, I know exactly what that feels like, because that's what I experienced when I knew I had outgrown religion. I realized that my freedom was under attack, and I either had to break free from the chains that were holding me captive, or continue to repeat the negative behavioral patterns that I still see in my family members and in so many others to this day.

I knew that there was nothing wrong with God or His love for me. The conflict was being created by the nonsense I was being taught in church. I simply did not want to be in a system that could not handle the truth, based on facts, not fiction.

I knew I could no longer follow blindly, and be abused along the way. That was unacceptable to me, and I couldn't go along with it any longer. But through all of that abuse and negativity in my youth, I never lost my love and passion for the people.

At times, I had to take hard blowbacks for saying things that most of the church members knew, but were too afraid to say themselves. I am a son of the church who is on the outside because I refused to play the religious game, which meant that I would have to totally surrender my life to its ideas, concepts, and dogmas for the balance of my life, without ever researching for myself what is true, and matching that truth with my own experience.

Freedom is the new heresy because leaving organized dogmatic systems of religion behind means reclaiming your God-given identity to see and think freely!

That is why God asked Adam, "Where are you?" Because Adam, by putting on a fig leaf, relinquished his identity to dress like the source of his new information— the Tree of the Knowledge of Good and Evil. Freedom is being able to take those clothes off in order to see your brothers and sisters as they truly are.

That is why we have been lackluster in life, just meandering around as if we have no purpose and no mission to accomplish in life. We have to get up off our knees, and stop waiting for the by and by. We have to reclaim our identity and begin to see ourselves as worthy again!

Freedom is the new heresy because so many people are awakening to their true identity. They are reclaiming that identity from religious institutions, realizing that those institutions are an impediment to real spiritual growth and development. The abuse that I was navigating through as a child showed me early on that there was something seriously wrong with the church's interpretations of scripture.

In the past, I was constantly thinking how unhealthy it was for religion to be so negative. We were using God to justify abusive behaviors. That is why husbands were so readily able to disrespect their wives and their entire families, and no one ever corrected it, because we were taught to be silent about those patterns of psychological abuse.

Those patterns of abuse resulted in my brother losing his life. The constant abuse of power and authority eventually provoked him to be angry, which led to him being thrown in the street by our stepfather, whose patterns of abuse went unchecked simply because the institution was more valuable than "real lives"! And we celebrated the very leader who pushed my brother to his death through abuse.

We have all sorts of dysfunctional families in the "kingdom," with dysfunctional, psychologically abusive, prejudiced, intolerant, and hateful messages and practices. And they are affecting the insiders and the outsiders. Yet, none of our most profound, proficient generals in the "kingdom" are willing to speak up or out about it!

That is because narrow-minded religious people never preach the truth when they profit from lies! And there are too many who profit from and off ignorance. The church members celebrate the leaders because the leaders have created welfare systems that always require the people to need the system. Never under any circumstances are the church members released from their bondage to be and become who God wants them to be in the world.

The teachers, doctors, lawyers, entrepreneurs, filmmakers, marketing executives, musicians, artists, performers, landowners, scientists, mathematicians, and inventors whom our communities need to rebuild have been stagnated by the primitive dogmatic beliefs of organized religion, setting generations of young people back by disenfranchising them from an economic future.

My message has never been about leaving God or abandoning faith to become a heathen nation! My desire is simply for people to abandon man-made constructs of God to gain Christ Consciousness. When we do that, we will be ready to mature in every aspect of our lives. We will grow spiritually not merely out of necessity, but with a new enthusiasm, knowing that we all deserve the best that the universe has to offer. With love at the center of our lives, we all have hope and a future. Jesus' message was considered heresy in His day, because He had to challenge the religious leaders of His time.

Here I sit, right back in the same neighborhood where I asked God why outsiders were presumably going to Hell because they didn't share my beliefs. Right here in Brownsville, Brooklyn, I am writing this book with the hope that my words will answer that question.

My neighborhood is totally changing and being reconstructed today. Everything in it and around it is becoming new and even getting new names. Yet, the church in which I asked about outsiders going to Hell sits in ruins, just a relic of what it used to be. There is no life there! No real love! No enthusiasm! No purpose! And many other churches have met the same fate. Many people die with narrow-minded religious delusions. During their lives, they mouth false platitudes while sticking to religious rituals and routines. They never have a genuine impact on the communities they were sent to serve.

Narrow-minded religious people have become an infection of bad ideas and bad concepts, robbing so many individuals of their true identity and purpose on Earth. They have made freedom a selling point for their religious communities, while never allowing true freedom to flourish. That is why people are abandoning the churches in droves, since reality is where it's at. Those churches have much catching up to do.

The fact that it was so easy for my religious leaders to dismiss me the moment I began to ask questions and think for myself tells me that it was my identity they were after. They were not interested in me as a freethinker who learns to live through my divinity. Rather, they wanted me to conform and give up my real identity to accept the one they created for me.

That is why they believe there is such a thing as church clothes. There are *no* church clothes! There are only clothes that they insist should be worn for church. But who are they outside of their fraudulent identity? Who are they if they don't go around judging and condemning the world?

And as long as they continue to see freedom as heresy, and a right that should be denied or controlled by them, they stagnate an entire culture of people, never allowing for a real experience of Christ Consciousness. Unfortunately, few people are telling them that they are so primitive in their understanding of God that they are no longer considered psychologically sound.

Their delusions have caused them to spend centuries trying to relive the Biblical days—hence, all their liturgical garments, as if they are in the Roman age or an episode of *Game of Thrones*. They are afraid to take ownership for their lives and truly accept what Godliness is. Instead, they audaciously deny God's power and refuse to allow others to experience it.

By the way, I no longer use the Bible as a guide for my life. I know that is shocking and appalling to some readers, but let's clear something up: nothing that has been touched by man can be considered infallible. Period! We can add or take away from scripture what we wish, but that doesn't make our interpretations correct.

Just because something is in the Bible doesn't mean that I have to make it a rule for my life. In talking with my Bishop, who was 72 at the time, with half a century of so-called ministry under his belt, I asked, "Bishop, what does the word *Bible* mean?" Not only could he not answer, but neither could his church leaders.

Those people claim that they lead us to Christ, yet they never even took the time to look up what the word *Bible* means. How is that possible, when they use the Bible to demonize entire groups of people and to justify their manipulation and control of their followers? They have planted churches all around the world, using the Bible as their defense. Yet, they have never even taken the time to look up the meaning of the word!

But many may say, "So what? What's the big deal?" That shows the ignorance of people and how their delusions have made ignorance acceptable and praiseworthy. They have used a book to dominate people's lives with religious servitude, and yet never even taken the time to surround themselves with the facts about it. That is not praiseworthy, it is totally unacceptable—especially when one considers how heinous a weapon they have made out of the Bible.

Just because something is in the Bible does not make it law. We must give up that primitive thinking and put the Bible in its proper place. Even Jesus taught us that.

> *"You have your heads in your Bibles constantly because you think you'll find eternal life there. But you miss the forest for the trees. These Scriptures are all about me! And here I am, standing right before you, and you aren't willing to receive from me the life you say you want. I'm not interested in crowd approval. And do you know why? Because I know you and your crowds. I know that Love, especially God's Love, is not on your working agenda. I came with the authority of my Father, and you either dismiss me or avoid me. If another came, acting self-important, you would welcome him with open arms.*

> *"How do you expect to get anywhere with God when you spend all your time jockeying for position with each other, ranking your rivals and ignoring God? But don't think I'm going to accuse you before my Father. Moses, in whom you put so much stock, is your accuser. If you believed, really believed, what Moses said, you would believe me. He wrote of me. If you won't take seriously what he wrote, how can I expect you to take seriously what I speak?"* (John 5:39-47)

Damn! We could close this chapter right there. The point couldn't be any clearer. Jesus paints a vivid picture of today's church and explains just how much of an impediment it is to a real relationship with Christ! If someone famous were saying this, everyone would be ready to receive the message.

The Bible is not where you find eternal life. Putting the Bible down and experiencing God is eternal life. Relying on the Bible is why we are still hearing boring, fanciful sermons that attempt to interpret Hebrew and Greek scriptures. Yet, those interpretations provide no practical everyday wisdom, knowledge, or understanding, coupled with principles to produce the magic and creativity of our divine design. That is exactly why freedom is the new heresy!

> *Christ has set us free to live a free life. So take your stand! Never again let anyone put a harness of slavery on you.* (Galatians 5:1)

Chapter 15

Completely Other!

Making the simple complicated is commonplace;
making the complicated simple, that's creativity.
　　　　　　　　　　　　　　　　—Charles Mingus

I₀ WAS EXTREMELY important to me to close this
book with this chapter. "Completely Other" is how I
have come to describe the message that I teach, because
I understand that it is totally different from what you
hear in traditional religious settings. That is why it is
sometimes difficult for people to accept, even though the
truth of the message is so liberating.

That is the core or essence of cognitive dissonance,
which occurs when the fundamental ideas that you have
always held as truth are challenged, and the actual truth

sounds foreign because lies have become your defensive norms. You defend those old ideas out of fear, even though their effects on your life are debilitating. So, I understand why my message of freedom may offend some people, or seem to others to be too good to be true.

> *I can't believe your fickleness, how easily you have turned traitor to him who called you by the grace of Christ. By embracing a variant message! It is not a minor variation, you know; it is Completely Other, an alien message, a no message, a lie about God. Those who are provoking this agitation among you are turning the message of Christ on its head.* (Galatians 1:6-7)

Paul literally describes in this passage how narrow-minded religious people have adopted a variant message—a message that is "completely other" from what God intended for our lives. Most of the sermons that are preached to us in religious settings are not even based on common sense. The preachers have simply learned to mask their folly and ignorance behind theatrics and show.

These false messages never challenge people to grow past the need for their religious fix. The preachers give them just enough of an addictive high to keep them coming back, week after week. I have even heard people say, "I'm gonna be doing this the rest of my life!" They actually have the audacity to call this religious addiction "honoring God," assuming that the false messages are God's directives for their lives.

Those negative messages are a dumbed down version of God's truth. They give us excuses to never grow into who God truly wants us to be. When we relinquish to others the authority that God has given solely to us, we allow those others to shape and dictate our lives. Thus, we never mature to the point of being responsible for ourselves.

My message is alien to many people, but ignorance is required to ignore it. In order to be in fellowship with false Christian messages, one must relinquish one's common sense and personality at the door. False churches are basically designed on the following premises: "Leave the real you at the door, and we will show you what you should be, how you should dress, how you should love, whom you should love, to whom you should give your money, with whom you can sleep, and with whom you cannot sleep. Give us your mind, and we will tell you how to think! We will tell you when to think! And don't ever think more than the middlemen! Don't ever be smarter or wiser than the shepherds. If you do, God will kill you!"

Many people have adopted this fickle teaching as truth and have levied this nonsense on the rest of the world in the name of God. They have turned the Gospel of Christ on its head! That is why American culture celebrates hypocrites—people who take on titles without having any genuine purpose. God's purpose for us is and always should be spiritual growth and development. God does not want us to be dazzling church workers, who lord our beliefs, philosophies, and dogmas over others. Rather, He wants us to take His love and demonstrate it in the world.

God wants us to teach others how to realize their divinity and infinite creativity. God wants us to awaken to our intellectual and cognitive abilities. God wants us to be freethinkers who know that life is not happening *to* us, but *through* us. We are co-creators in our own experience. But many of us would rather preach nonsensical messages that foster fear, hatred, and intolerance.

Those hateful messages tell lies about God, who never sent His Son to rob us of our identity and originality. He sent His Son to restore those to us! He was not looking for clones bound to someone else's opinions, ideas, and interpretations of what He wants for us. The odd thing is, my perspective is not new. Paul had to deal with these same issues centuries before I came along.

By accepting watered down, regurgitated, fanciful sermons as truth, people have accepted the bondage and all the adverse effects that come along with their delusions. Let's take a look at those things again that Paul described in the Book of Galatians.

> *It is obvious what kind of life develops out of trying to get your own way all the time: repetitive, loveless, cheap sex; a stinking accumulation of mental and emotional garbage; frenzied and joyless grabs for happiness; trinket gods; magic-show religion; paranoid loneliness; cutthroat competition; all-consuming-yet-never-satisfied wants; a brutal temper; an impotence to love or be loved; divided homes and divided lives; small-minded and lopsided pursuits; the vicious habit of depersonalizing everyone into a rival; uncontrolled and uncontrollable addictions; ugly parodies of community. I could go on.* (Galatians 5:19-21)

In this passage, Paul has perfectly portrayed today's Christian churches. All the sins named above are exactly what the so-called "kingdom" has become. Sadly, narrow-minded religious people realize it, but in their delusion they choose to ignore it. They have been begging God stagnantly and repetitively for revival, because that is all they know to ask for. But revival is basically requesting God to restore the past.

Revival brings back to life what is dead. Revival is not what today's churches need. Today's churches need an awakening! They need to be awakened to the truth! They need to be honest about the lies they have created. Religious leaders can no longer be our heroes to whom we go for spiritual wisdom and counsel.

Narrow-minded religious people have lived a dumbed down faith because of their foundational untruths. Their ignorance and refusal to become independent freethinkers enslaved them to lies and deceptions. They have become the evil while pretending to be the good.

Freedom is costly, and should not be squandered on religious rituals. Religious middlemen must be exposed for who they are, and their idolatrous images must be torn down from the pedestals built for them.

> *I said it once; I'll say it again: If anyone, regardless of reputation or credentials, preaches something other than what you received originally, let him be cursed. Do you think I speak this strongly in order to manipulate crowds? Or curry favor with God? Or get popular applause? If my goal was popularity, I wouldn't bother being Christ's slave. Know this—I am most emphatic here, friends—this great Message I delivered to you is not mere human optimism. I didn't receive it through the traditions, and I wasn't taught it in some school. I got it straight from God, received the Message directly from Jesus Christ.* (Galatians 1:9-12)

Many people may find it weird that I am challenging today's so-called religious leaders. But that is precisely what Paul tells us must be done, regardless of reputation or credentials. Those middlemen must be held accountable for the lies they have created in God's name. In our pursuit of God, we have allowed people to lead us who have never genuinely experienced God. Thus, we have become a generation of the blind leading the blind. Consequently, as a community, we continuously fall into ditches.

I am so grateful for the leaders who do make love the center of their message. As I have stated earlier, I'm sure that many of those leaders have nothing but great intentions for the people. However, their religious system will not allow room for any new and fresh thought. Furthermore, those leaders who have love at the center of their message are often demonized by the religious elite for not being condemning enough.

Like Paul, I did not get this message from any human authority. Nor did I learn it in school. It came to me directly from the Source and has always been totally beyond my control. Clearly, I am not writing to strengthen the religious traditions I grew up with. To the contrary, I am writing to insist that they be torn down, and from their ashes a new people will rise, who will live out their divinity, and the works of their hands will be infinite.

> *Jesus then left the Temple. As he walked away, his disciples pointed out how very impressive the Temple architecture was. Jesus said, "You're not impressed by all this sheer size, are you? The truth of the matter is*

> *that there's not a stone in that building that*
> *is not going to end up in a pile of rubble."*
> (Matthew 24:1-2)

Today's institutional church is as transitory as the temple that so impressed Jesus' disciples. Nevertheless, narrow-minded religious people brag about how big and pretty their house of God is. They claim that anyone who is not in it does not have the Spirit of God. That is their attitude toward all outsiders, as they believe that their institution is protected by God.

Jesus said basically, when Christ Consciousness arises, not one stone of that temple will still be lying on another! The whole thing will come crumbling down, because Christ Consciousness is not about bricks and mortar. It is an awakening of and to "Oneness," which does not require bricks and mortar, only surrendered hearts.

Christ Consciousness does not require religious slavery. The sheer essence of the religious worship practiced by narrow-minded religious people promotes separation from God, because in telling God how great He is, they diminish their own value. But one cannot ascribe worthiness to God before first ascribing it to oneself. Seeing yourself as one with God does not require you to adopt the primitive belief that you are separate from God.

Our message should no longer be about salvation and the cross. I know some of you think that I have made up that idea, but it actually appears in the Bible:

> *Therefore leaving the principles of the doctrine of Christ, let us go on unto perfection; not laying again the foundation of repentance from dead works, and of faith toward God, Of the doctrine of baptisms, and of laying on of hands, and of resurrection of the dead, and of eternal judgment.* (Hebrews 6:1)

How have we missed this? Why is salvation from Hell the only message of the institutional church? We should have left that doctrine behind centuries ago. Yet, narrow-minded religious people are still stuck with those same old messages, imprisoned by the doctrines of eternal judgment and the laying on of hands! They are still throwing people under baptismal waters who never get up and live out love, which is the infinite expression of God on Earth.

Have I mentioned the spiritual and financial poverty that narrow-minded religious people have accumulated, due to their watered down spiritual principles? They must stop practicing delusions in the name of God. They have bragged about how many years of service they have given to the church and how faithful they have been at showing up for services. Now it is time for them to show up in the world.

What has the so-called "kingdom" of the institutional church produced? Condemnation? Blind following? Conformity? Living life vicariously through Biblical characters? When will narrow-minded Christians practice Christ Consciousness, rather than promoting their interpretations of scripture, telling others what they think the Book of Revelations means, or what their pastor preached last week?

When do narrow-minded Christians show up in the world as themselves, with all their original brilliance? When do they get to experience the love they talk about so much—without judgment and condemnation? The institutional church has taught such self-hatred that it has made loving others virtually impossible. Why? Because the alien message of the church teaches separation. You can only love what you deem holy, sacred, and lovable.

The message of the institutional church is "completely other" from the real message of Christ. So-called sacred houses of worship are actually the very Antichrist against which they preach. Hebrews 6 tells us to move onto perfection. But what is it that we need to perfect? It's simple. We need to perfect love!

> *There is no fear in Love, but perfect Love drives out fear, because fear has to do with punishment. The one who fears is not made perfect in Love!* (1 John 4:18)

A fear-based Gospel does not represent or come from God. That requires no debate. "Perfect Love drives out fear!" Yet, the institutional church proposes that people must fear punishment, for God has designed Hell for them. Narrow-minded religious people have not been perfected in love, and therefore they cannot lead us in love. Instead, God is raising a remnant from all walks of life, who have broken away from the institutional church or even never experienced religious slavery at all. That remnant will become the leaders of the New Way.

I know it may be a difficult pill for narrow-minded religious people to swallow that God will actually raise up people they consider the least deserving. But it happens and will happen more frequently than they think. In fact, let's look at the very chapter in the Bible that they cite to lead people to salvation.

> *So the big question is, Why didn't Israel understand that she had no corner on this message? Moses had it right when he predicted, When you see God reach out to those you consider your inferiors — outsiders! — you'll become insanely jealous. When you see God reach out to people you think are religiously stupid, you'll throw temper tantrums.* (Romans 10:19)

The institutional church has no monopoly over the message of Christ, which is not bound to any religious denomination or preacher. The message of Christ does what it wants, reaches whom it wants, when it wants! No one has the right to hold it hostage to Sunday morning and once during the middle of the week.

I totally understand how some people may think that what I'm teaching sounds a bit strange. But what I'm teaching *must* sound strange because it is totally different from what most people have been taught. Those institutional church middlemen have never had any intention of leading people to find their own true identity. They are blind guides who need to be totally dismissed and forgotten. Jesus taught the same message to his disciples:

> *"These people honor me with their lips, but their hearts are far from me. They worship me in vain; their teachings are merely human rules...."*
>
> *Then the disciples came to him and asked, "Do you know that the Pharisees were offended when they heard this?"*
>
> *He replied, "Every plant that my heavenly Father has not planted will be pulled up by the roots. Leave them; they are blind guides. If the blind lead the blind, both will fall into a pit."* (Matthew 15:8-14)

Like Jesus, I must warn against modern-day Pharisees, who believe they are the righteousness police. Clearly, I did not come up with this message myself. It has always been there, for Jesus Himself tells us that every plant that His Father has not planted will be pulled up by the root!

Jesus did not say to abandon only the Pharisee middlemen, but also those who followed them. And he told us why: "If the blind lead the blind, both will fall into a pit." We who are awakened and becoming awakened to the truth must abandon the righteousness police and begin to forge a new way through Christ

Consciousness! Those who choose to remain in their delusions can continue to remain in their pit, like blind sheep led to slaughter.

The message that narrow-minded Christians have built their lives on is totally contrary to what Christ desires for us. Those nursery rhymes preached in the institutional church, backed by a Hammond B3 organ, have numbed us to Christ's real purpose for us, which is love. That is exactly why my message may appear a bit strange. It is Completely Other, for freedom is the new heresy!

Made in the USA
Middletown, DE
26 September 2020